Clothing's Value
Beyond The Price Tag

Valerie Gross

CIP data on file with the National Library and Archives

Print edition: ISBN 978-1-55483-548-5
E-book edition: ISBN 978-1-55483-549-2

For all those who have inspired my passion for textiles, the design process, and who have taught me so much about style and quality clothing.

And for Lyle, who appreciates fine clothing, and who cherishes all the hand-knits made for him over the years.

May your closet be filled with clothes that truly represent who you are.

Table of Contents

Introduction

"Fast fashion is the opposite of a world in which we buy better but less. It is the utmost example of selling more and worse." J.B. MacKinnon

Everyday, millions of people ask, *"What am I going to wear?"*. Those closets staring at us are stuffed with clothes, many of which will have a short lifespan. The amount of thought that goes into answering this daily question surrounds the nuances of our habits, occupations, social activities, and the weather. But nary a thought is given to where our clothes originate from, and why so much of our clothing is inexpensive and of low quality.

Whether or not you have an interest in fashion, there is meaning to the clothing that lives in our closets. Clothing is a basic tool of communication and a form of self-expression. Clothes convey something to the world about who you are, your occupation, your social and economic status, and your self-worth. Zara, the first fast fashion retailer, and all the others that followed, is when we see an increased acceleration in clothing production, but also introduced something new - *disposable fashion*. The speedy delivery of trendy, cheap fashion into the stores was made possible by offshore manufacturing, and fashion's addiction to synthetic fabrications. We have developed an insatiable appetite for inexpensive goods.

Prior to the 1990s, excessive amounts of clothing were not produced; people were more adept at making things last as long as possible, and respected their relationship with clothing. In our quest for cheap, we have little attachment to the clothes hanging in our closets, often tossing them in the trash long before they are no longer useful.

I have a passion for fashion. In fact, my background in clothing and textiles is one of the reasons I decided to write this book. However, the issues of excessive production, over-consumption, and textile waste have gnawed at me for a long time. My interest in these topics began in the early 2000s co-inciding with the rise of fast fashion. I thought it would be a simple task, I set out to replace my worn out black wool pant suit with a new version. However, I was frustrated to find that I couldn't find anything made of 100% wool. All I could find were blended fabrics, with synthetic polyester the predomi-nant fibre in the mix. As someone with a background in tex-tile science and knowledge of fibre properties, to not find clothing that contained mostly of natural fibres, and that would last longer than a season, bothered me to no end.

I'm also frustrated with the overuse of the word *trend*. Ironically, trends are the lifeblood of fashion, loosely defined as the general direction in which fashion is developing. The initial stage in the lifecycle of a fashion product is the intro-duction of a trend. Most trends or those referred to as "*fads*" are short-lived, and the ones that survive move through the market until they are of no interest, or become classics that cycle in and out of fashion. Today, this is where fast fashion lives; retailers and manufacturers continuously flood the mar-ket with trends, on a monthly, weekly, and even a daily drop for some companies like Shein. This hypercycle of trends, the endless speed and constant newness has greatly in-fluenced our shopping habits.

Trends are so out of control that the distinctive styles of fashion have become blurred. Unlike previous decades of the 20th century when specific styles defined an era, it's now more difficult to pinpoint characteristic fashions among the main-stream, due to the volume of products available. You could swap an actor's attire worn in a Seinfeld episode from the 1990s, wear it today and scarcely notice a difference. It could also be argued, that everyone adopts similar looks, with an increased danger of losing personal style and individuality.

The business model that pervades the fashion system is one of year over year profitable growth to appease investors and shareholders. Fast fashion has been grossly lucrative for the entire industry. Costs trump all other concerns. How the fast fashion companies accomplish this is through excessive production, constantly cycling through trends, which are often artificially invented by the companies themselves. The products from this type of manufacturing are made cheaply and lack in quality, thanks to subcontracting offshore and synthetic fabrics. And luxury houses have not been immune from excessive production. The luxury market is a victim of its own success, as many of their products are no longer based on scarcity or exclusivity. They like to tell us that it's because we demand these products, but producing more clothing than we could possibly ever wear, it is unrealistic to think that any consumer would ask for this scale of production.

Psychologists agree that the more we are exposed to this type of overstimulation and excess, the less it thrills us, and as something becomes cheaper we want more of it. Anything but mindful, we have succeeded in diminishing the value of clothing. Our relationship to clothing is broken. Do you know who made your clothes? Where? How? Do I really need that blouse in another colour? We think nothing of wearing something only once. Maintenance is not part of our vocabulary, and many people lack the skills to repair or upcycle garments.

Television and fashion journalists have always had an influence on our choices, but today social media and the marketing messaging from companies are heavily intensifying our compulsion to overbuy. Have you heard of "*fast fashion hauls*" presented by influencers on YouTube or TikTok? They are nothing more than a shameful display of conspicuous consumption; pretty young women presenting boxes filled with poor quality items purchased at ridiculously low prices without a thought to the materials, quality, manufacturing processes, or the plight of garment workers. Stylists, social media influencers, and many of us measure a garment's worth by its price tag alone.

The excessive production and consumption of cheap, low-quality clothing and accessories, and the effects of fast fashion are nothing short of disastrous. Beginning in the 1980s, contracting clothing manufacturers offshore created massive labour lay-offs and trade deficits in North America and Europe, shifting business structures from design and manufacturing to the design and marketing of brands. The burden is being shouldered by the people in the global south who make our clothes (80% of which are women), communities overwhelmed with fashion's waste, and fashion's heavy toll on the environment.

We have reached a tipping point. We are beginning to realize that we need to be more connected to the process of designing and making clothes. The demands for change towards sustainability are obvious by the victims of fashion's damaging practices, including the environment and humans. The industry needs a reboot to minimize its footprint, with a system that balances social, economic and environmental needs. If you love fashion, learning about the true costs of fast fashion is a wake-up call.

This book does not provide a detailed analysis of the toxic effects of fashion production. Instead, it offers information and tools that give us the knowledge to make better clothing choices, and mend our relationship with clothing (no pun intended). I will take you on a journey that examines the materials of our clothing, the meaning behind what we wear, fashion's sustainability challenges, the ingredients of quality clothing, and how to create a more conscious wardrobe. To make much needed change begins with an understanding of how we reached this critical point, by examining the evolution of the fashion system.

Chapter 1

The Fashion System - Then & Now

"Fashion is not something that exists in dresses only; fashion is something in the air. It's the wind that blows in the new fashion, you feel it coming, you smell it. Fashion is in the sky, in the street, fashion has to do with ideas, the way we live, what is happening." Coco Chanel

Today, mainstream fashion clothing is divided into three broad categories; luxury brands with high-profile names, such as Chanel, Prada, Armani, Marc Jacobs and Louis Vuitton. Some of these companies continue to manufacture haute couture alongside their ready-to-wear and accessory collections. Next comes the crowded space of mid-market brands such as J. Crew, Banana Republic, DKNY, Armani Exchange and other designer diffusion lines. At the bottom is low-cost clothing which primarily consists of *"fast fashion"*, a highly profitable segment with a sophisticated marketing machine and highly efficient production processes. The whole system of fashion is now designed to produce, market and consume clothing for the capitalistic motive - making money.

Mass production of fashion clothing is nothing new, but what is new is its unprecedented scale. During the Industrial Revolution at the turn of the 20th century, advances in productivity, and the invention of the sewing machine, brought dramatic increases in clothing output. Before this time, most clothing was made in the home, or custom-made by professional dressmakers and tailors. These professionals produced made-to-measure clothing from the styles and trends that trickled down from couture houses. Clothing was not discarded as readily as it is now, and when it was out of fashion, it was gifted, altered or recut. Ready-made gowns from the fashion centres of Paris, New York City, and London were available in specialty and department stores for wealthy clientele.

In the 1900s, the first ready-made clothing available were basics, such as underwear and shirtwaists, a popular blouse style of the time. Clothing manufacturing expanded greatly during this decade. Fast forward to today, and now we purchase most of our clothing off-the-rack or by its more popular term, *"ready-to-wear"*; clothing that is mass produced in a factory setting. Custom-made clothing is now rare among middle-class consumers.

The 1990s introduced a new business model for clothing production, marking the rise of fast fashion. Fast fashion describes cheaply made clothing and accessories, based on current trends, and their speedy delivery from the runway to the stores. Today fast fashion accounts for the largest proportion of clothing sales globally. Precipitated by globalization and technology, it is common for most of the processes of clothing production to be outsourced, including some of the products made by luxury brands. Fast fashion relies heavily on outsourcing to keep costs low. Changes in fashion styles, technology, and cultural shifts have led to an increasingly complex and fragmented supply chain, in which production processes are contracted or subcontracted out in all brand categories. Fashion's history explains how this happened.

Haute Couture

I'm watching the series *Emily in Paris*, oohing and awing over the clothing worn by the actors. For over a century those interested in fashion have been enamoured by the originality and creativity of haute couture and luxury fashion. Ever since the beginning of what the western world refers to as *"fashion"*, Paris has been revered for its skill and beauty of their textiles and clothing. Like the delicious French food found in even the least desirable looking restaurant, most French people walking the streets are ever so chic and elegant, just like the actors in *Emily in Paris*.

In its early days, wearing fashionable clothing was the prerogative of the rich and leisured, as they were the only ones who could afford luxury clothes and keep up with the changing styles of dress. Ready-to-wear was produced on a small scale, and manufacturers of women's fashion obtained designs from various sources: purchase of fashion forecasts, illustrations of seasonal designs, colours, and textiles, and the most widely used method, *"copying"* haute couture. Copying and diluting haute couture garments for mass markets continues to this day. Fast fashion brands copy designers, producing *"knock-offs"* made in inexpensive fabrics to be sold in chain stores.

Around 1850, the Englishman Charles Frederick Worth is credited as the father of French Haute Couture in Paris. He was a couturier, and a highly influential designer. He began his career in French fabric houses, and while he was at Maison Gagelin, his wife began wearing his designs. Soon customers were requesting his work, and eventually Worth opened an establishment in 1858. Worth attracted the attention of elite women because of his use of lavish fabrics and trimmings, the incorporation of historic costume elements, and his attention to fit. His success is attributed to attracting the patronage of influential women including Empress Eugenie of France. Soon all of fashionable Paris waited in his showroom.

He developed a new business structure for fashion clothing, selling his designs wholesale to foreign dressmakers and stores, for adaptation to their clientele. High fashion began to be associated with designer names rather than the clients who wore their clothing. This *"trickle-down"* effect of high fashion begins with Worth.

Worth's sons expanded his business into the Chambre Syndicale, the organization of couturiers that still regulates and promotes French Haute Couture, under its new name Fédération de la Haute Couture et de la Mode (FHCM), representing both women's and men's haute couture.

Worth helped Paris to lead international fashion, and today Paris is still a major fashion capital, and home to all haute couture houses.

During the early years of the 1900s, other influential factors helped Paris maintain its unchallenged supremacy, through the creative talent from other fields of art. There were often collaborative efforts between fashion designers and artists. Chanel designed for the Ballets Russes in 1924. The Art Deco design movement which originated in France in the mid-to-late 1910s, had a strong influence on the clothing and jewelry styles of the 1920s and 1930s. The French government continually encourages the arts, including fashion.

What is haute couture exactly?

The literal translation of haute couture is *"high dressmaking"*. A fashion house or designer atelier creates exclusive garments that are often trend setting fashions tailored specifically to a client's measurements. This custom fit high fashion is constructed by hand from start to finish. The fabrics are of exceptional quality, and sewn with great attention paid to fine details, such as beaded textiles and handworked buttonholes.

In France, *"haute couture"* is a protected name and is guided by strict rules originally created by the French government in 1945. *"Couture"* is often used loosely to describe any garment that is hand-made, one-of-a-kind, or original. But to qualify as haute couture, a house or designer must comply with the rules to earn haute couture's prestigious label.

The minute ready-to-wear garments were introduced to the masses in the early 20th century, haute couture's relevancy began its decline. Historically, many predicted its death, but like a classic piece of clothing that endures the test of time, haute couture may not be as viable, but is in a constant state of flux. Part of the reason for this is the labour intensive nature of haute couture, which renders it available to an incredibly small market who can afford this type of luxury. There were around 1000 clients worldwide in 2018, with 80% of sales to wealthy Chinese, and the remainder reserved for red carpet events, and other global clientele.

Its viability is certainly tested in a world of relaxed dressing, and our insatiable appetite for trendy cheap clothing, where consumers freely crossover by mixing expensive and lower priced products - jeans meet a luxury tailored blazer. Today, haute couture is primarily a marketing tool, relying on other sources for revenue. Haute couture exists to capture the imagination, and reinforces a brand's legacy of the craft. It's undeniable that haute couture sets new trends for ready-to-wear. Digital images gives enjoyment to the masses, and provide design teams from fast fashion brands and others, with popular looks to interpret and manufacture. It also serves as research and innovation for new fabrics and technological development.

Haute couture houses or designers are required to present collections as dictated by the FHCM. There is an exclusive allocation of tickets or an entrance fee to view these collections. Although the costs to produce a show are enormous, the collections are viewed as a laboratory of free expression, or visual art displays, without the constraints of commercialism. Most of the marketing budget comes from the money earned from other licensed products.

The most well-known haute couture houses include Chanel, Dior, Prada, Versace, Hermès, Louis Vuitton, Gucci, Fendi, Valentino, and Giorgio Armani. Once ready-to-wear was firmly established, it wasn't profitable for haute couture houses to make only custom-made fashion, so they diversified into ready-to-wear lines and other luxury products. Today, haute couture houses have varied business models:

designers from established ateliers that present at Paris Fashion Week, small independent house designers with no huge advertising budget that possess a strong international client list, and the groups who practice conceptual fashion or rather more artistic clothing.

The Industry of Luxury Brands

During the 1950s the couture trade noticeably declined. As a response, couture houses diversified into luxury products and specialty boutiques containing *"pret-à-porter"*, or French ready-to-wear collections. Pret-à-porter or high quality ready-to-wear was seen as an alternative to *"factory"* clothing, which was associated with poor quality and primitive design. In 1966, Yves St. Laurent, who began his career in the House of Dior opened the first boutique Saint Laurent Rive Gauche. This marked the first time that a French couturier successfully launched a pret-à-porter collection. In 1971, St. Laurent announced his final couture collection. By the late 1960s, the major couture houses including Chanel and Givenchy started pret-à-porter collections.

What we are seeing today is that the characteristics of the prevailing linear business model have infiltrated luxury houses, forcing them to overproduce. Jean Paul Gaultier has been quoted as saying *"Too many clothes kills clothes"*, in response to the hectic production cycle, which resulted in him quitting the design and making of ready-to-wear collections.

The luxury industry produces and sells not only clothing, but also licensed products such as leather goods, footwear, silk scarves and ties, timepieces, jewelry, perfume, and cosmetics. Most luxury brands bear the name of its founder - Louis Vuitton, Chanel, Gucci, and Prada. Many of these businesses are now owned and run by business tycoons of multinational conglomerates. The largest and wealthiest conglomerate, LVMH Moet Hennessy is owned by Bernard Arnault. LVMH owns over 75 companies. The conglomerates spend millions on their brands, and haven't been immune to the ills of capitalism.

The luxury sector does not rely exclusively on the sale of expensive clothes to make a profit, but relies on licensed mass produced commodities. Christian Dior was licensing items such as handbags and hats as early as the 1950s. Most luxury brands started as exclusive, small one person shops selling handcrafted, artisanal merchandise made from the finest materials. Louis Vuitton began his career as a designer and artisan of leather made trunks for high society, due to the popularity of train travel in the mid 19th century. Coco Chanel was a skilled, and original couturière who liked to use humble fabrics to create relaxed and elegant high fashion.

Luxury clothing began as exclusivity, made specifically for the wearer, and designers developed close relationships with their clientele.

Today, luxury brands follow a pyramid business model of production and sales. At the top of the pyramid is the most exquisite work by traditional artisans, made in limited quantity in France, Italy and the UK. These luxury items, including haute couture are sold to wealthy customers. The manufacture of mid-range pret-à-porter, or high quality ready-to-wear bearing the name of the famous designer or brand, is outsourced to large factories closer to home in places like Spain, North Africa and Turkey. The lower end products of the luxury pyramid including T-shirts with logos, knitwear, and denim are produced mainly in China, and other areas like Mexico.

There are only a handful of luxury companies that remain independent, and have bucked the trend of mass production dictated by corporations. One such brand is Christian Louboutin, a small designer owned footwear company. You may be familiar with his signature red soles. He has succeeded through design integrity, and a devotion to his high profile clients.

The focus has shifted from the creative design process of making exquisite clothing, to that of profit, and the belief that everyone deserves a little luxury. This is achieved through licensing their luxury name on anything and everything, and selling to the middle market. Some would argue that luxury fashion is now too uniform, and has lost its cachet through overproduction and heavy licensing - "*fast luxury*". At one time, Pierre Cardin produced only haute couture, but then he resigned to focus on ready-to-wear in the 1960s. Cardin is notable because at the time he was the most highly licensed designer, putting his name on everything, none of which he designed. He has often been accused of "*trashing fashion*", but he certainly tarnished the Pierre Cardin image. Unless you are a fashion history buff, one can't identify him as contributing to fashion in a meaningful way, because his name was diluted to the extreme.

Canada's Fashion Industry

Documentation of the history of Canadian fashion has lacked a certain enthusiasm. The focus of attention has been on the cities of Paris, New York and London, because haute couture and designer high-end clothing have a rich history in these centres. Since Canada and the United States have comparable standards of living and market-oriented economic systems, and the fact that the US is our largest trading partner, our fashion histories evolved in a similar way. Our similarities include the propensity for copying European styles, and the belief that Parisian fashion is superior. But it took Canada a much longer time than the US to break the copying habit set by manufacturers, and to visualize the potential for the exploitation of the designer label.

During the 19th century, Canada was developing as a country while Europe already had an established and growing fashion industry. Canada imported technological expertise from abroad to develop its textile industry, and facilitate the production of fashion. With an increasing population and rising family income, the demand for garments increased.

The roots of the Canadian fashion industry were in the cottage industry. The first manufacturing companies were established around 1868 in the cities of Montreal and Toronto. In Montreal, the garment district originated on Bleury Street, St. Peel Street, and St. Catherine's area, and on Spadina Avenue in Toronto. The primary product manufactured was coats.

Between 1870 and 1900, there was a change from hand-tailored to factory-made garments because of technological developments and the invention of the sewing machine. Initially, men's suits were mass produced in Canada, followed by dresses, blouses, foundation garments, sweaters and millinery. Canadian census records from 1870 revealed that most of the garments were cut in tailor or wholesale clothing shops, and then distributed to homeworkers to be sewn. The problem of inconsistent quality, led to the entire production process being done in a factory setting. Therefore, the manufacturing of basic items was well established in the 19th century.

Due to our close economic and political ties, interest in Canadian women's fashion was influenced by the British during the late 19th century. During this time of British influence, wealthy Montreal women consulted British journals for the latest available trends and styles. Generally, women in North America kept abreast of trends by either travelling to Europe, or reading illustrated pattern books and magazines. Eventually, they looked to Paris and New York for fashion information, as status dressing was important to this segment of society.

Because of the styling complexity of garments at the beginning of the 20th century, the years between 1890 and 1915 were important for dressmakers of women's clothing. During these early years of the 20th century, dressmakers were inexpensive to commission, relying heavily on copying Parisian looks for their clients in large city centres, like Montreal. Like the Americans and British, Paris designers were considered the most prestigious by Canadians. Canadian high society women required appropriate clothing for a variety of functions. Through their ability to travel, they could commission couturiers in Paris, purchase ready-made in American department stores, or patronize Canadian dressmakers.

Ready-made clothing, especially basic items became more available to consumers in the first decade of the 20th century, but most women's clothing was still produced by home sewers, dressmakers or tailors. Sewing skills were included as part of home economics education programs for young ladies. The Toronto City Directory of 1901 listed 150 tailors, and approximately 550 dressmakers in business. Many of the tailoring and dressmaking establishments were competitive with the world's fashion centres. Around 1900, Timothy Eaton began manufacturing for his department stores. Some firms also developed in the Hamilton-London, and Kitchener areas, mainly producing work clothes, hosiery, and knitwear. Winnipeg, Manitoba also became a major garment manufacturing centre, along with Toronto, Montreal and Vancouver.

The first World War changed women's lifestyles and their wardrobe needs. There was a redirection of the female labour force into the manufacture of weapons, and other military essentials. Uniforms and overalls were necessary for these working women. Also during the war years, women were encouraged to repair and restructure existing garments. Even after the war, this interest continued with women's magazines offering articles on how to recycle existing garments. Thriftiness, frugality, and practicality were essential characteristics of women's clothing choices.

For women who could afford luxury clothing, exclusive Canadian retail stores carried both originals and exclusive copies to promote sales of Parisian styles. Specialty shops in department stores such as T. Eaton & Company (Toronto) and Oglivy's (Montreal) took custom orders for designs in their salons. Other major department stores included Simpson's, Morgan's, Holt Renfrew, and Woodwards in Vancouver. Since the late 19th century, "*piracy*" or copying of designs was a common practice, precipitated by fashion plates and magazines. International fashion trade was disrupted during WW1, with fashion catalogues suggesting that customers allow substitution for the lines illustrated, because manufacturers couldn't guarantee a continual supply of garments.

With the emancipation of women in the 1920s, Canadian clothing manufacturers began to offer a wider range of ready-to-wear options for working women. The prosperity of the growing middle class, advances in technology, and the introduction of rayon and simpler designs, made it easier for manufacturers to copy and emulate fine fabrics. Manufacturers either employed sketchers to travel to couture shows and draw the originals for copying, or purchased fashion magazines to predict styles and colours. The simpler styling details of clothing also allowed home sewers, and rural dressmakers to easily make clothes. Designs were filtering down from couture to the cheaper levels of production, making them available to more Canadian women. Despite these changes, tailoring businesses prospered, with some dressmakers in Montreal, Toronto and Vancouver achieving notoriety.

In the mid-1930s, the reality for manufacturers in Britain was that copying Parisian couturiers practically guaranteed market success. They were reluctant to hire a designer to create original styles or promote design talent. This strategy also proved successful for North American businesses.

The Canadian women's fashion industry actually began in the latter part of the 1920s and 1930s. During this time, Gaby Bernier, a couturière set up a salon on Sherbrooke Street in Montreal, which lasted 25 years. Gaby Bernier is historically significant because she is probably the only, and earliest Canadian couturière to have presented a successful collection, albeit only once during her career. Gaby Bernier felt that couture fashion shows would not work in Montreal because of the costly nature of the event, few backers to support the show, and nowhere near the numbers of clientele needed to support couture. Instead, she chose to participate in group fashion shows. She also felt few Canadians were daring enough to wear imaginative clothing because of their conservative and dignified nature. When Bernier had her salon, it was difficult for Montreal designers to achieve recognition because of limited press coverage, a problem that still exists for many Canadian designers.

The depressed economy of the 1930s saw a move towards traditionalism, but there was still a desire for status dressing, influenced by Hollywood actors. Many manufacturers went out of business and those that survived implemented cost saving measures, including relocating to Montreal where cheap, non-union labour existed. Fewer stores imported original designs, and instead produced less expensive copies. The depressed economy of the 1930s increased the production of ready-mades to meet the demand for reasonably priced fashion clothing. Customers continued their interest in Paris fashion news, and dressmakers were still abundant in Canadian cities, including Gaby Bernier, and another prominent couturière, Marie-Paule Nolin.

In the 1940s, banks and the government became interested in promoting the fashion industry, deeming "*fashion*" sales more profitable than selling "*clothes*". Canadian Business magazine from August, 1946 reported that little was known about the industry as there was no established means of advertising. Although some sources indicated that the Canadian industry was thriving with sales of women's wear reaching $140 million in 1943. The industry in Quebec was highly developed, with many small establishments. As a result, the Montreal Fashion Institute was formed to deal with what was felt to be a poor perception of Canadian goods. The War Time Price and Trade Board imposed its A61 clothing regulations, forcing manufacturers to consider product changes for the domestic market. By controlling all aspects of the price of goods, supplies, and services to the Canadian public, the government was able to ensure an adequate supply of clothing, therefore avoiding the need to ration clothing. Despite regulations, fashion changes occurred, specifically in the category of women's wear.

Stephen's 1949 article in Canadian Business stated that high profile designer names do not make the "*big money*". The giants of the Canadian industry are those manufacturers which mass produce low priced cotton house-dresses for their durability and quality. The article goes on to indicate that much of Canada's "*look*" is foreign inspired, but mentions that Canadians are good at items like skiwear. Other authors suggested that professional marketing firms were essential for the promotion of ladies wear. Few Canadian designers set styles for others to copy, and manufacturers needed an incentive to develop a Canadian fashion consciousness amongst women.

With the growth of manufacturing in the 1940s, there was a need for designers. Some Canadian design houses opened including, Lawrence Sperber and Alfandri in Montreal, Rae Hildebrande and Louis Berger in Toronto, and Rose Marie Reid in Vancouver. However, many manufacturers continued to copy as many designs as possible, claiming difficulty in resisting advertising from the United States and Europe. During WWII, Holt Renfrew carried Marie-Paule Nolin's designs, but resumed copying Paris haute couture after the war. As a result, Nolin left Holt Renfrew. A promotional film about Canadian fashion designers was released in 1946, but name recognition did not emerge like it did in the US. Due to the lack of communication from Europe during WWII, Americans were forced into finding their own style direction, marking the beginning of American designer promotion.

North American consumerism took a strong hold in the 1950s. Consumerism embraced a marketing strategy, that sought to determine what customers want, and then sold it to them. European designers reigned supreme with American designers starting to make a name for themselves. Canadian designers were relatively unknown, but in 1954 Raoul-Jean Fouré founded the Canadian Association of Couturiers, which lasted for 10 years. The Association held shows in

New York to promote Canadian textiles and designers. The New York based Fashion Group Inc. formed regional associations in Montreal and Toronto to promote cooperation within the industry.

English fashion in the 1960s was highly influential. This time period proved to be a turning point for Canada's fashion image, with manufacturers employing Canadian designers. There was a surge in the industry because of a new generation of trained designers, Margaret Godfrey for Bagatelle, Leo Chevalier, and John Warden. John Warden produced uniforms for Expo 67, exposing Canadian fashion to the world. The federal government promoted the talents of Canadian designers by sponsoring fashion events in New York to stimulate interest and sales.

Prior to the 1970s, Canadian fashion displayed a heavy reliance on copies or knock-offs from Europe and the United States. Another common practice was to manufacture authorized line copies. However, in the 1970s consumers became obsessed with the status that came with designer labels, precipitated by increased media reporting of fashion. In spite of previous marketing tactics, manufacturers began to see a reason to exploit the Canadian designer label, as consumer spending was increasing.

Increasing technology in the 1980s changed systems for designing and producing goods and services. Companies started flirting with "*just-in-time*" production, where a certain proportion of their products were being made in low cost centres. By virtue of their small size, Canadian manufacturers were recognized for producing design-oriented quality goods, because of their advantage of flexible short production runs. The last decades of the 20th century and into the 21st promoted many Canadian designers: including Alfred Sung, Jean-Claude Poitras, Simon Chang, Hilary Radley, Linda Lundström, Wayne Clark, Lida Baday, Club Monaco, and the group Comrags. The Toronto-based Fashion Design Council of Canada was established to promote Canadian fashion.

In the early 1980s, Canadian manufacturers found it difficult to compete because of the lower production costs in developing countries, import regulations, the North American Free Trade Agreement (NAFTA), and increased outsourcing of work. The growth of cheap imports from Asia and the US, directed Canadian talent into high style, and quality niche markets. My theses research found that small firms received higher profitability if they made a commitment to design, whereas profitable large firms were least committed to design. This was because larger companies catered to a wider mass market, and their well-developed systems of production increased the importance on cost and speed of delivery. For large companies, focusing on design creates higher production costs with a decrease in profits.

The problems faced by the Canadian fashion industry in the 1990s included advances in technology, changing global patterns, rising production costs, declining retail sales, and free trade. Companies competed on the basis of quality, rather than price to develop a strong brand. During this decade, my research found that the majority of Canadian fashion companies were vertically integrated, performing the functions of design, manufacturing, and retail in-house. Generally, Canada fell short of high quality fabric suppliers, and expensive European fabrics were sourced because it was possible to purchase small quantities. To have products manufactured in China was difficult because small orders were often denied, or it was required that a company own other stores to meet manufacturing quotas. Because of offshore outsourcing by many of the large retailers, small companies placed greater emphasis on making high quality products, and less of a focus on price.

Geographically, Canada is a vast country, sparsely inhabited, and is the second largest land mass in the world with a population that recently hit the 40 million mark. The Canadian market is relatively small with varied lifestyles and vast distances between markets. Canadian fashion tastes have been reported as conservative without an interest in high style. We were said to have a knack for adapting foreign styles to our likes, and due to our climatic conditions, we excel at producing practical clothing.

Today, the nature of the domestic market is fashion conscious, and Canadian designer clothing possesses an imaginative fashion orientation. But Canadian designers have not always been recognized by an identifiable look, as our American neighbours have. Perhaps this is because of Canada's size, market differences, the many different sources of inspiration, and the fact that small business size is a reality for fashion apparel companies in Canada.

Small business size is a reality for most Canadian fashion designers and manufacturers. Canadian cities abound with small, local design companies that offer quality, and now more sustainable fashion options. Companies like Lululemon and Roots are recognized around the world, and there are many amazing outerwear companies like Mackage and Canada Goose. Meghan Markle has even been spotted wearing a Mackage coat. In early 2023, Mackage opened a flagship store in Paris; a milestone for a luxury Canadian outerwear company to compete on the world stage. There are also low cost retail chains filled with trendy inexpensive clothing like Le Chateau, Garage, Suzy Shier and Joe Fresh, but most aren't owned by huge conglomerates as in the US, Europe or the UK. Canadian malls consist of the same fast fashion retail chains found in the US and Europe including H&M, Zara and Uniqlo. Many Canadian fashion companies still design in-house, but produce in low cost countries, as well as locally, depending on the type of product.

America's Fashion Industry

Since the beginning of apparel manufacturing, the public has been enamoured by the glitz and glamour attached to American and European fashion. Studying fashion's history in the western world, is inevitably the study of American and

European fashion. Their major cities are the birthplace of the apparel industry, and of technological advances which accelerated the production and sales of fashion worldwide.

The early days of garment manufacturing in the US produced two types of clothing; practical basics, such as undergarments and work clothes made in large factory settings, and stylish clothing made with high quality materials and skilled labour. Fashionable clothing was cut and sewn in the lower east side of New York City. Working class men's and children's clothing could be purchased ready-made from the mid 19th century. Because of the standardized nature of men's and children's garments, manufacturers could produce them in bulk without fashion changes.

Because New York was America's busiest port, it is the birthplace of the apparel industry in the US. European fabrics came through this port, but it was also the immigration point for Europeans looking for work. Many of these immigrants were highly skilled in needlework. New York City became the financial centre for investment in a growing apparel industry. In 1900, the garment industry was New York's largest employer.

Stylish fashion was inspired by or copied from Parisian couture houses. Since the late 19th century, piracy of fashion designs has been established and widely practiced method of acquiring style ideas and trends. This was made possible through the availability of fashion engravings and photographs in pattern books and magazines. In the early 1900s, department stores sent employees to Paris Fashion Week to covertly sketch designs presented at shows, and these were manufactured as *"Paris Originals"*. Luxury houses went to extreme lengths to try to deter the practice, but copying permeates the fashion industry to this day. Today we use the term *"knock-offs"* to describe a fashion product that evokes the original by having a similar appearance, but without the use of a registered trademark. Knock-offs are copies of products that manufacturers find inspiring, or interpretations of designer trends. These products are made with lower quality materials, without the fine details of high-end clothing, and are usually sold at cheaper prices than the originals which inspired them. An old practice, but copying is now a highly profitable strategy for fast fashion companies.

During the late 1800s and early 1900s, wealthy American women patronized couturiers, and commissioned designer custom made garments, especially dresses, much like their counterpart in Canada. Lower class women either sewed their own clothing or sought the service of dressmakers. Women still made a great deal of clothing at home for financial reasons, utilizing catalogues and magazines for trend information.

Rayon fabric was introduced in 1910 by the American Viscose Company, and was accepted as a silk substitute, for its similar drape and hand. This allowed manufacturers to emulate top quality fabrics at a fraction of the cost of silk.

For the first time in the 1920s, the essence of couture was adapted and translated for mass production. Lesser fabric requirements, the simplicity of designs, and loose fitting, tubular shaped styles of the 20s enabled manufacturers to easily copy high fashion. The styles were also suitable for both working women and the elite. Coco Chanel introduced fabrics like knit jersey into couture collections. Prior to this time, these humble fabrics would never have been worn by wealthy, fashionable women, but by using these types of fabrics, Chanel was able to create an elegance that women embraced. Ready-to-wear was becoming increasingly available to the masses.

As the industry grew in New York, manufacturers moved to midtown Manhattan, which became known as the Garment District, consisting of a vast network of showrooms. By 1931, NYC had more apparel manufacturers than anywhere else in the world. The 1930s depression years resulted in couture houses losing their export market to the US. However, there was a silver lining, with a new fashion focus for North Americans - the clothing worn by Hollywood stars. They were highly influential and copied by North Americans and Europeans. The overall trend in ready-to-wear for the middle class moved towards economy and convenience, luring customers away from the dressmaker and tailor.

Fashion was toned down during the second world war, with factories focusing on uniforms and wartime essentials. Post war, an economic boom initiated a return to producing fashion. American designers made a name for themselves during the latter years of the war. The system of mass manufacturing and retailing expanded, and ready-to-wear began its domination.

There were changes in how fashion was manufactured. The fabric was cut in Manhattan workrooms, and the cut pieces were trucked outside of the city to be sewn. Trucks brought the finished garments back to the showrooms and warehouses, and then the finished goods were sold to retailers. This process of cutting and sewing in different locations led to the fragmentation of fashion's supply chain - a precursor to the massive amount of outsourcing prevalent today. Eventually, the Garment District was replaced with designer fashion studios, which designed fashion clothing and farmed out the sewing to neighbourhood factories. NYC is still a fashion design hub, but not for garment manufacturing.

In the 1950s, society embraced commercialism. The manufacturers of consumer goods increased by 60%. Dual income families were increasingly common, and the rise in income expanded the market for goods and clothing. New technological developments, and the introduction of nylon after the war, commonly used in underwear and hosiery, drove an interest in synthetics. High quality ready-to-wear clothing grew, and teenagers began to adopt clothing different from what their parents wore, influencing the move towards casual clothing like jeans.

In 1955, Mary Quant opened Bazaar on Kings Road in London, heralding the dominance of boutique shopping in the 1960s. Bazaar stocked Quant's own designs, creating demand for fashion clothing at more affordable price points. The 1960s counterculture revolution, and mainly English designers radically changed the business of fashion. Fashion was British-led during this period, beginning with Quant, and London became a major fashion centre. Quant expanded her brand by developing paper patterns for Butterick Sewing Co., and had her name on a variety of products including cosmetics.

For centuries, fashion in France had been based on the trickle-down effect; haute couture for the elite, copies for the upper middle class, and diluted couture for the mass markets. Now fashion was originating from the streets, and haute couture didn't have the same influence as in prior decades. The economic pressures forced French houses to expand into ready-to-wear.

Boutique style shopping fueled the idea of having the right fashion and access to the latest looks immediately, and at affordable prices for the customer. These niche designer retailers created a conducive selling environment aimed at the young; filled with pop music, a self-service approach, and modern interiors. Beginning in the 1950s, mass media plays a major role in creating demand for goods and services, increasing consumption rates to keep up with production. The notion of *"obsolescence"* was built into consumer products, and clothing was one of the easiest products to accelerate turnover.

The 1970s became synonymous with designer name dropping, and consumers developed an obsession with labels. The label is a highly effective marketing tool, spreading the allure of a brand. High profile couture designers, young French designers who started ready-to-wear lines in the early 70s, and English designers created excitement and awareness of their brands. Labels and logos began to appear as signatures on accessories such as scarves and bags. Manufacturers realized the power and prestige of brand names.

High profile American designers of the 1970s included Bill Blass, Geoffrey Beene, Mary McFadden and Oscar De La

Renta, primarily known for dressy day and evening wear. Elegant and wearable sportswear trends were established by Halston, Anne Klein, Ralph Lauren, Calvin Klein and Perry Ellis. Consumer spending continued to increase, particularly within a new target market - *"the yuppie"*. Fashion collections were presented twice a year, *Spring/Summer* and *Fall/Winter*, with some companies producing a resort collection at the end of the year. Milan, Italy became a new fashion capital, and in 1975 Giorgio Armani led the pack of influencers, a designer of ready-to-wear for both men and women.

We tend to think of sustainable fashion as part of the new green movement, but *"eco-fashion"* first appeared in the 1970s, as part of an environmental movement associated with *"hippie"* culture. The emphasis of hippie culture was on self-sufficiency, and wearing natural textiles. Their clothing often consisted of second-hand garments and handcrafted designs. More often, this type of fashion was equated to shapeless, drab-coloured garments made of hemp, cotton, or linen.

Initially, companies produced basic garments like shirts overseas, but quality was difficult to control in the early years. Important technological changes of the 1980s included CAD, which stands for computer aided design. The laying out of pattern pieces and cutting fabric was traditionally performed by a skilled pattern cutter. With the implementation of CAD, the process was made more efficient, and prior to cutting, pattern pieces were laid out using this design program, to minimize fabric waste.

During the 1980s, the US Apparel Manufacturers Association organized, and on the agenda was how to compete against low-cost markets. *"Quick Response (QR)"* and *"Just-in-time"* concepts were introduced, which affected the production of fashion clothing. Increasing technology changed the systems for designing and producing goods and services, but also in terms of time and ability. New looks were tested through focus groups before submitting orders for production.

Initial orders with these technologies were small and frequent, and reorders were based on whether or not the sales data indicated a demand for them. The goal was to cut the amount of inventory on hand. By increasing turnover of high demand products, companies could avert seasonal leftovers that would typically need to be marked down. In an ideal world, the supply chain would run more efficiently, at lower costs, with minimal waste, and fewer losses. Customers get what they want, at the right time.

Initially, QR systems were not fully embraced by manufacturers, as it was a steep investment for small companies. Those that participated triggered an initial spike in American products and the desired drop in imports, but this did not last. This marked the *"undoing"* of apparel manufacturing in the US. It became increasingly impossible for the domestic market to compete with foreign competitors, who were already using this type of production.

Another major upheaval in the domestic apparel manufacturing industry was the expiry of the Multi-Fibre Arrangement (MFA), established in the 1970s to set quotas and preferential tariffs on apparel and textile imports to the US, Canada and Europe. From 1974 to 2005, the MFA tried to limit the amount of imports from developing countries through quotas, but instead enabled China to build huge factories to meet the high volume of orders. The finalization of NAFTA in the 1990s also changed the textile and apparel manufacturing industry, with millions of jobs lost. This marked the beginning of the democratization of luxury brands and the highly competitive business of fashion, where the costs and speed of production are the most important criteria for business success. The best strategy to realize high profits in this highly competitive market was to move from onshore to offshore production. That's exactly what many brands did in the 1980s. Countries for manufacturing purposes were often chosen based on having lower wage costs, weaker labour movements, and lax environmental regulations. The traditional clothing strategy that designed and marketed clothes in-house was usurped by outsourcing.

Fast Fashion - The New Business Strategy

It's difficult to pinpoint the exact beginning of fast fashion, because mass production of clothing has existed since the late 1800s. The late 1980s and 1990s experienced the rise of a business model adopted by retailers. This strategy expedited production and distribution of short fashion runs, based solely on copying the trends and silhouettes of luxury and designer brands. The scale of production and technological advances changed and accelerated over time, allowing for this business model to entrench itself. Trend-based fashion is produced in inexpensive, low quality fabrics, without the fine details and skilled techniques used to make high-end clothing. The shorter manufacturing cycle of goods meant that seasonal sales were unlikely, and increased the pressure on consumers to buy frequently - what we call "*fast fashion*". Brands embraced a pure capitalistic model based on volume and high profits.

Fast fashion relies on aggressive pricing strategies so that they can move large quantities of inventory at low prices, rather than small quantities at high prices. Companies accomplish this by chasing the lowest bid, so they can slash retail prices and maintain high profits.

You may never have heard of Ortega, the founder and owner of Inditex, the largest fashion group in the world. But chances are you have patronized their most profitable and successful fast fashion retailer, Zara. Zara is credited with being the first fast fashion company. Amid the Covid pandemic's increase in e-commerce sales, China's Shein online fashion platform surpassed Zara and H&M fast fashion sales in the US. Up to this point Zara was the most successful of the fast fashion retailers.

In 1975, Amancio Ortega and his wife started Zorba, a small fashion clothing boutique in the port town of La Coruna in northwest Spain. They had to change the store's name to

"*Zara*" because of another business with the name Zorba, located in the same area. Zara at the time was a classic ready-to-wear business, showcasing seasonal collections of trends or knock-offs manufactured in Spain. In these early days, the turnaround time was approximately six months.

In the 1980s, like other global ready-to-wear designers who were considering QR or the application of digital communication technology, Ortega made the decision to implement a new design and distribution method. He wanted to merge speedy production processes with retailing to rev up the amount of trends showcased, and increase sales and profits. Initially, he produced locally so the clothes could reach the stores quickly, be sold, and then restocked immediately. Ortega called his new business system "*instant fashion*". By 1989 Zara had 85 stores in Spain. As Zara grew, and the demand for clothing increased, the family started to outsource in Morocco, close enough to Spain to manage quality control, and still maintain fast delivery of products.

Other competitors and early adopters of this model joined in the race during this time period, including GAP, H&M, Benetton, and Urban Outfitters. All of these brands began to copy styles from the top fashion houses, manufacturing them cheaply, and offering them at ridiculously low prices. The brands that adopted this highly efficient production process became known as "*fast fashion*". During the finalization of NAFTA in the 1990s, western governments negotiated trade deals that encouraged offshore production to take advantage of cheap labour. China's apparel exports multiplied, and they developed huge factories that would only produce high volumes of clothing. From this point we see the proliferation of fast fashion retailers.

By 2001 Zara had 507 stores worldwide, with a turnover time from the design process to the sales floor in 5-6 weeks. In 2001, the parent company Inditex went public on Madrid's Stock Exchange, and by 2018, Zara had a total of 2200 stores in 96 countries. Inditex also manages other brands, including

Zara Home and Massimo Dutti, and as of 2018 all their stores totalled 7400 across 96 countries. Today, Inditex can ship new items to all their boutiques and e-tailers twice per week, an incredibly short period of time.

Zara has a highly efficient supply chain and inventory system. The latest designs are copied from the collections presented at shows in NY, Paris and Milan, and translated into inexpensive clothing sold in Zara retailers across the globe in approximately 15 days - a non-stop cycle of refreshing and replenishing clothing stock. How does Zara manage to achieve this incredible level of productivity?

In Thomas's book *"Fashionopolis"*, she indicates that on average, shoppers visit fast fashion stores 4 times per year, but for Zara it is an astounding 17 times per year. In a Zara outlet, if a style doesn't sell within a week, it is pulled off the sales floor, and any standing orders are cancelled. If the sales data suggests an item is popular, a small number are manufactured locally in Spain, Portugal or Morocco. Then after a month or so, the item is replaced by a new look.

The international market value for fast fashion is forecasted to reach 133 billion US dollars by 2026. There are other players besides Zara, including H&M, Sweden's multinational; UK's Topshop, Boohoo, and Pretty Little Thing; Primark, headquartered in Dublin, Ireland; Japan's Uniqlo; Fashion Nova; Mango; Massimo Dutti; and the latest entrant Shein.

Today the fashion supply chain is highly fragmented, turning out clothing that is nothing more than hand made goods broken down into assembly line steps. Each of the steps of the production processes: weaving, knitting, dyeing, cutting fabric, sewing, applying notions, and additional finishing details are contracted or subcontracted out. This system has infiltrated high-end and luxury fashion houses, forcing many of them to adopt this kind of scale to compete with fast fashion companies - companies that only design and market clothes in-house, and outsource production. For the most part, the demand for cheaper and cheaper clothes has succeeded in wiping out both the Canadian and American garment manufacturing centres.

So what have we been left with? Fashion's linear system has turned clothing into a disposable commodity along with a myriad of sustainability challenges - pollution of the environment, tons of clothing waste, and human abuses. Our closets are stuffed with clothes that leave us feeling more than unsatisfied, and rarely are we in touch with clothing's ingredients. The system has altered our relationship with clothing, so much so that clothes are only sustainable to us in terms of cost alone. What does it really mean to value clothing?

Chapter 2

Clothing is More Than a Commodity

*"...I think it's funny when decades and things are just the
current thing...Everybody wants to be somebody else,
rather than using those images as a stimulation to look at
themselves and redefine and redesign themselves and see
who they are." Carmen Dell'Orefice*

In the late 1980s and early1990s, I watched three one-half
hour television shows every Saturday. Each reviewed the latest fashion trends in clothing, art, architecture and home
decor - CNN Style with Elsa Klensch, Fashion TV with
Jeanne Beker, and Fashion File with Tim Blanks. The latter
two hosts are important icons in the world of Canadian fashion
and style. Like an art enthusiast, these shows were a source
of entertainment, fascination, and inspiration, but I never felt
compelled to own everything that was presented to me.

The pace of changing fashion styles, known as "*trends*",
is so fast today that these types of TV shows wouldn't be able
to keep up with the amount of fashion information we are
bombarded with, from social media and the internet. With the
advent of fast fashion retailers and their hypercycle release
of trends, the moment they hit the airwaves, they become almost irrelevant before being replaced by the next trend. These
niche shows don't exist anymore, and have been replaced by
shopping channels, style segments from celebrities, influencers, professional stylists, and magazine editors.

The effects of fashion production have not only intensified the climate crisis, but have also altered our relationship with clothing. It might seem to observers that fashion is now more about fitting in, rather than a form of self-expression and feeling good about our clothing choices. We spend so much time shopping, that we're less fulfilled with our purchases. We are less connected to the people who make our clothes, ignorant of the materials used to make them, unaware of the production processes, or where our garments are made.

Fashionable clothing once dominated by Parisian designers, was only accessible to the wealthy. Western clothing styles once unique and handcrafted became more simplified. With the help of technological developments beginning with the sewing machine, mass production of clothing became possible. The ready-to-wear industry grew over the decades accelerating the speed of fashion changes, and leading to a market overrun by fast fashion retailers, and a new entry, "*ultra-fast fashion*". Clothing should have value and a purpose beyond our insatiable appetite for all things new and inexpensive. It's how we've come to interpret our clothing that has diminished it's worth. There is meaning to the clothing we adorn ourselves with daily, how we respect ourselves and others, and what we are ultimately saying to the world.

The Meaning Behind Clothing

You might be thinking that in light of our increasingly troubled times, clothing is frivolous and inconsequential. What scholars agree on is that people in all cultures modify their appearance, and clothing, a material object is one example of this modification, which serves an essential function in our daily lives. Clothing is so basic, that we often don't attach meaning to what we're wearing. But the life of clothing hardly ends as soon as it is purchased - the woven, knit, stitched and dyed fabric will be with us for a long time.

At its most basic, clothing is for protection and practicality. Throughout history clothing served other purposes. It differentiated the sexes, designated age, marital and socio-economic status, identified membership within a particular group, and had ceremonial use. Clothing reveals a great deal about society, a silent language that tells the onlooker about the organization of a culture.

Clothing is not only practical but has aesthetic value. In our culture it's a matter of looking good, but also what is socially appropriate and what is considered fashionable. The amount and type of clothing we wear varies according to the standards of modesty in society. We probably wouldn't wear a bikini to go shopping for groceries, and most of us would feel out of place doing so. Historically, we were taught which body parts to conceal; Victorian women could not expose ankles, but could expose décolletage. And to some degree we wear clothes to enhance our sexual attractiveness.

The clothes we wear are a consequence of the society in which we live. What we wear, and how we wear our clothes is socially learned, and inherently expressive in nature. Clothing is a non-verbal form of communication, but has limitations without language cues. The communication revealed by clothing can take place through already established meanings. For example, clothes may act as signs, or rules that society attaches to them, such as the placement of men's and women's buttons; women's buttons are placed on the right side, and men's on the left. Clothing signs express an individual's social identity, including gender roles, class, status, occupation and group affiliation. Individuals interpret clothing signs, and apply their variations to these *"rules"* of appearance.

Clothing as a form of self-expression has its place in maintaining a positive self-image, a common identity, and communicating the activities of the wearer. Dress symbolizes changes that occur in societal values and attitudes. Clothing also reflects the political climate, technological patterns, and economic conditions of society.

It follows that styles of dress serve as a means of communicating personal and societal values within the context of each historic period. A style is the predominant form of dress in a given time period or culture. Throughout the 20th century it was easier to identify predominant styles of dress within a specific time period, and this is well documented by costume historians. These unique styles persisted for long or short periods of time. When ready-to-wear took over as the mainstream business model, style innovations accelerated, driven by mass production and the media. With the inception of fast fashion, the distinctive styles blurred. It's difficult to pinpoint characteristic styles among the mainstream, because there is so much clothing out there from which to choose.

What is fashion?

The word fashion is really an attribute with which some clothing styles are endowed. Fashion influences what we wear, what we like, and is a large part of the social world in which we live. Everyone has thrown out clothes in good condition because they are out of fashion. We are constantly met with references to fashion, surrounded by brick and mortar stores and online retailers. We are also fed an enormous amount of fashion "*news*" or information. We judge clothes and others by means of fashion standards, and our tastes in fashion change over time.

Fashion is mainly used to refer to clothing and styles of appearance, but it is also found in other aspects of intellectual and social life, such as architecture, interior design, and even philosophy. The changes are slower in these areas than in fashion clothing. Historically, new ideas in art and home décor influenced the clothing fashions created by designers.

The word "*trend*" is overused by the fashion industry, and is defined as the general direction in which fashion is developing. Fashion is about change for change's sake, and the illusion of novelty. This is the heart of any fashion business, and the lifeblood of fast fashion retailers. The fashion industry is not only concerned with the production of clothing, but also with producing new trends and style innovation. Fast fashion concentrates on generating profits from pumping out trendy-based fashion over design and style innovation. These companies leave the style innovation to the original designers, who I might add are often short-changed or unrecognized for their talents.

The meaning of fashion has changed over the years, mostly because of the non-stop cycle of refreshing and replenishing stock with trend-based fashion styles. Luxury brands were forced to adopt a similar scale of production, to compete with fast fashion.

Fashion is no longer a line handed down from Paris, as in the days of Dior, when originals were only made available to the wealthy. This luxe image of fashion lost its cache, and now it could be argued that fashion simply means "*clothes*". Clothes which are heavily marketed by ad campaigns, promoted by celebrities, stylists and journalists through their highly subjective recommendations. Why do we need several versions of the same style? Why do we need a new coat every winter?

Economic growth is the central guiding principle in capitalist societies, and generating profits is what the fashion industry is about. Consumers continually buy, discard and incite low-end retailers to continue manufacturing at an unprecedented scale. We've become passive consumers with too many clothes, and a disposable culture with little respect for the items hanging in our closets. Fashion is now driving overconsumption, rather than allowing changes to move slowly and intentionally through the market.

How did fashion develop?

The word "*fashion*" became synonymous with "*style*" after the late 14th century, when rapid changes in clothing styles began to emerge. It's said that fashion developed with the breakdown of feudalism, the rise of capitalism, an increasing population in towns, and the introduction of fitted clothing.

Under feudalism, dress was linked to one's rank and position in society. Heredity dictated your stance in life and the styles you could wear.

In the late Middle Ages, society changed because of a number of events including the Crusades, which helped to bring new products from other parts of the world. Most significantly, there was a growth in trade between Europe and the Middle East, and an increasing population. The growing class within towns made their living from crafts and commerce. The developing merchant class amassed great wealth from new ideas and imported products.

New styles of dress were possible through increased social interaction and mobility within towns. By the 16th century wearing clothes that were not in *"fashion"* was a sign of inferiority; fashion was an indicator of status and social orientation. With the continued development of urbanization and industrialization, the ideal stage for fashion was set. This could only happen in societies that were changing economically and politically. The growing complexity of society, and the succeeding Industrial Revolutions (technological and digital) led to the mass production of clothes, making fashion more widely available to all.

Why Fashion Changes

The last section describes how fashion came to be, but why does fashion change? There are a variety of explanations for why fashion changes, some carrying more merit than others. The trickle-down theory described fashion change in its earliest days, whereby styles spread vertically down the social hierarchy. The upper income groups adopted fashion first for its exclusivity and symbols of distinction, followed by the lower classes emulating these styles. At a certain point, the upper classes discarded styles they no longer felt were in fashion. They took up new styles and the process repeated itself. Trickle-down theory depends on a lag in adopting styles. Haute couture houses kept styles secret for personal customers who could purchase and wear them before they were released to the public.

Today, people from all levels of society wear fashionable clothes. The fashion industry introduces new styles each season, regardless of whether a previous style has worked its way through the social hierarchy. People still have a desire to imitate others, especially the fashions worn by influencers and celebrities.

As fashion has evolved over the decades, it is no longer the socially prestigious who decide when a new style will come into being. Clothing styles created by designers and manufacturers go through a selection process in collaboration with retail buyers, and is not predetermined by what the wealthy have chosen, but rather by what each brand stands for. This process determines what is available to the public as fashion.

We are in the age of conspiracy theories, and one view is that designers, manufacturers, and retailers work together to introduce new fashions, forcing consumers to accept what's offered. On the surface, it might appear that this is what's happening, because some items never return to the marketplace. Designers and manufacturers are in competition, and they all don't make the "*new look*". A change in fashion can either make or break a business. The public decides in the end which design ideas to accept or refuse. Given the structure of the fashion industry, a sustained conspiracy is highly unlikely.

But, there is a hierarchy of sorts within the fashion industry. The designers at the top of the pyramid (luxury brands) provide the lead. Other designers and manufacturers look to them for ideas, and these ideas are used as inspiration, or for copying. Of course not all ideas are generated at the top, but by a variety of groups in society. Styles such as workwear, sportswear, and clothing of ethnic groups have always been worn by various segments of society, and at times are introduced as fashion by designers.

Mass media helps to create and push change, through the immediate availability of photos online. Newspapers and magazines provide trend information; such as what styles to wear and how to wear them. The styles and trends aren't available and adopted throughout the marketplace at the same time. Consumers at each economic level don't behave uniformly. There are members in every group who are either fashion leaders, early adopters, those that purchase well-established styles, and those that don't really care about fashion.

Another theory is that individuals are responsible for fashion change. More often, one individual or designer alone cannot change the course of fashion, but rather is representative and influential of specific trends within fashion. Princess Diana was certainly fashionable, but she did not introduce a brand new item or create a new look. As for designers, they belong to a community, and can't help but be influenced by each other.

Scholars also suggest that changes in fashion are motivated because of boredom. This holds some truth, in that we buy new clothes because we grow tired of what we have. This can happen due to curiosity, a desire to be different, or for a variety of other reasons. There are other proposed views on why fashion changes, but what is agreed upon is that fashion now spreads across socio-economic groups moving horizontally, rather than vertically. People are heavily influenced by marketing. There are fashion leaders, followers, and deniers. Fashion has become something that changes over time, and something people ought to keep up with.

Relationship Breakdown

I love fashionable clothing, and like to be known for good taste and the ability to personalize my choices, put clothes together, and add my creative touches. I don't always get it right, but what's right anyways. I'm particular about how things are constructed, and the materials used to make them.

I enjoy clothing treasures from bygone eras. I'll never forget a 1920s, silk chiffon, beaded, and fringed flapper dress from the House of Chloe in my university's textile collection. Although treasures from the past show signs of wear, they do reveal the beautiful fabric that has endured the test of time, the attention paid to the stitches whether made by hand or a sewing machine, and fine details like embroidery or an inside pocket of a blazer. In previous eras, there was a respect and common sense know-how the owner gave to extend the life of each garment. This is an experience that most of those born after the 1990s may never know.

It follows that I feel a sense of loss for the pride that people used to have in wearing something special, either made by hand, or having saved up money to purchase a unique piece. An item that received love, enjoyment, and lasted a long time. Gone is the sense of quest. There is truly more to clothing beyond the designer label and the price tag. So how did we become so disconnected from our clothing?

Too Many Clothes. The largest factor affecting our disconnect is excess production and consumption. We are making and buying more than we could ever need, and more than the earth can possibly sustain. In the early days of fashion, when most of our clothes were custom-made, we respected and maintained them. Around the 1960s, when ready-to-wear took over as the mainstream business model, style innovations were launched and disseminated more rapidly. Historians noticed that fashion cycles increased, driven by mass production and the media. As we moved into the late 1990s and early 2000s, fast fashion retailers dramatically accelerated an already bloated production system. The market flooded with excessive amounts of fashion products, especially inexpensive, poor quality clothing and accessories. It's is hard to believe that during the Covid pandemic, ultra-fast fashion with even lower prices was introduced by Shein, China's largest online retailer. Luxury premium brands also produce excess, making products at a variety of price ranges, which are still more expensive when compared to the other clothing categories. Retailers of all types adopted fast fashion's retail strategy to varying degrees.

Psychology experts say that no matter how many more perks, rewards, material goods, or things we acquire doesn't make us happier. The boost in happiness from purchasing that "*it*" bag doesn't last long, resulting in us feeling a whole lot worse. The more we have to choose from, the more likely we compare ourselves to others, and suffer from decision fatigue. We have difficulty in understanding the difference between wants and needs.

The wide availability of fashion products has diminished that feeling of desire and anticipation of getting something new; it's so much easier to click the button. Remember when the hunt for that special something was a lot more fun. Fashion can simply be a source of inspiration for your own creations or like a great piece of art, a source of fascination; you don't have to own everything. And why bother saving up for something nicer or more expensive, when you can approximate the look very cheaply.

We tend to wear only a small percentage of what's in our closet. Sometimes clothes hang in the closet with tags still on, possibly never to be worn. Often we buy garments, simply to wear once or twice, then tossed. The lower price signals that a product is disposable. All this fashion sitting around diminishes its cache and value, making fashion nothing more than a commodity - to be bought and sold. Marketers like to make you think that you ask for stuff to be made. We didn't ask for fast fashion, but we certainly took to it with enthusiasm. When clothing is so inexpensive or marked down, people know they don't need it, but at 70% off feel it's worth it, and end up buying stuff they don't need. If you're a diehard fast fashion customer you shop more than other consumers.

How Clothes Are Constructed. New clothes have become so instantly available, that we've lost the deep connection to how things are made. The manufacture of fashion is labour intensive and consists of a series of steps, and today these production processes are performed in a number of different locations around the globe. Built into this system is planned obsolescence, a deliberate manipulation of the product's design so that it doesn't last long, encouraging repeat purchases. Because of this, we've lost the respect for the time and place in which things are created. There is no recognition of the original designer, or an appreciation for luxurious fabrics, and the skill required to make clothing. Ultimately, our expectations are lowered, and we are more willing to accept substandard products, considering only a garment's worth in dollars and its use, which is often only for a short period of time or just a few wears. People don't understand what makes for a good fabric, cut, or the fit of quality clothing. We've forgotten that clothing requires a great deal of work, but don't want to pay a reasonable price for it. The expectation for cheap inevitably hurts clothing designers.

Do you remember home economics in junior high school? I learned some basic skills like how to sew on buttons, hand-stitch a fallen hem, patchwork, and mend a small hole in a knit. I also learned how to cut and sew fabric pattern pieces, and learned which seams were the most appropriate for each section of a garment. These simple skills do help us understand the effort and work that goes into the design and construction of clothes.

Much of our fashion, particularly at the low-end is stitched together by factory workers who perform individual tasks, such as inserting zippers all day and inspecting finished work. Even these workers aren't part of the whole process of designing and constructing garments. They too are disconnected from the creativity and rewards from making clothes.

The Materials of Our Clothing. Did you know that Canada's Textile Regulations require that all clothing and textiles have a fibre content label stitched into the item? The disclosure label must indicate the fibre content (generic name) expressed in percentage by mass (65% polyester, 35% cotton), and the dealer identity. Care labels are also attached to clothing, and the information must not be false or misleading. Labels will typically indicate where the item was made, and more recently if the materials have met environmental standards such as Oeko-Tex certification. The fibres that make up fabric, reveal properties and characteristics about how a garment will stand the test of time.

Do you know the difference between natural and synthetic fibres? Most of the clothing for sale, particularly at the low-end consists mainly of synthetic fibres, like polyester made from fossil fuels or non-renewable resources. A disturbing statistic is that polyester alone makes up over 60% of garments on retail shelves. The reason for this is simple, the predilection of polyester over natural fibres keeps prices low. Consumers have been trained to think that synthetics perform better than natural fibres. For some products this is true, but the benefits are highly overrated. The following chapter provides the essential textile science information that will help you to make better clothing choices, but also to appreciate where your dollars are going.

Origins of Our Purchases. In fashion's early days, people had a relationship with the makers of their clothing, couturiers, dressmakers and tailors. Customer service was specialized, and the makers understood your needs. It was indeed a pleasurable affair, choosing the clothing from an intimate fashion show and being fitted by the creator. Ready-to-wear clothing at all price tiers changed all that. We either leave a store with brand logo bags, or we click a purchase button online and hope the item fits. But each experience now comes without specialized service.

Our insatiable appetite for fashion products has also made us blind to the suffering of garment workers around the globe. The ready-to-wear industry from its earliest days has been a dark one, and the ethics haven't changed much. We still exploit people who make very little money to produce ridiculous amounts of clothes. It's unfathomable that as recently as 2013, one of fashion's greatest tragedies occurred, the collapse of Rana Plaza in Bangladesh where over 1100 people died.

Making clothes is labour intensive, and sewing is one of the most common professions within the fashion industry, but also in the world. Labour is a large part of production costs. The wages that are paid to workers and to the factories greatly affect the cost of fashion. It follows that a market filled with cheap clothes needs cheap labour, and is the main reason why offshore outsourcing is so popular.

What isn't in front of us makes us blind. We don't see the amount of work that goes into making clothes, the poor factory conditions, or the environmental hazards workers experience. You can't possibly make a garment yourself for the price you pay in a low-end retailer. I knit the majority of my sweaters, and sometimes I pay over $200.00 for the materials alone, which doesn't include the hours spent knitting. One begins to see how ludicrous it is to pay $20.00 for a dress or $5.00 for a T-shirt at H&M, without thinking about the value of this work.

Who's really controlling our decisions? Although not ground-breaking, fashion has always been newsworthy. Since fashion became a thing, coverage has been geared more towards women, the most dynamic sector of the fashion industry. Before the internet, fashion information was controlled by fashion magazines, and their editors. They dictated their vision of where the direction of fashion was headed. Prior to the 2000s, defining trends could easily be identified, but now there are too many trends to count. Without fast fashion stores and affordable products, trends would not be able to spread so quickly. Because mass copying of styles is the prevailing business model, and trends sell clothes, this only increases consumer demand for new.

Today, the dissemination of fashion information has broken down, and is controlled by a bunch of rival style tribes, each offering their opinions, which only serve to intensify overbuying. These tribes include celebrities, professional stylists, social media influencers, and the like. Editors of fashion magazines are now beholden to their advertisers, and are focused on promoting the products of fashion corporations. We are given best dressed lists, red carpet styles, must-haves, and how to look like a celebrity with a high-low mix. We end up ignoring the evils of excess.

Fast fashion companies are marketing machines. Their marketing strategies are designed to get you to buy more, by rarely restocking older, popular items in order to lure you back for "*fresh*" merchandise. There's no finding that same item you adored for so long. The messaging through advertising is incredibly persuasive; what to wear, how to wear it, need for the latest trends, prioritizing price over quality, how to look like a celebrity for less, and why not engage in retail therapy, or shop your way to happiness.

The marketing strategy with the promise of designer bargains at a fraction of the cost of the original, kicked off in the early 2000s. Isaac Mizrahi designed a "*cheap chic*" collection for Target in 2002, Karl Lagerfeld for H&M in 2004, and others followed suit. These collections have nothing in common with high-end designer clothing. All these high profile designers signed off on sketches which retailers took to their manufacturers, who made the designs inexpensively without the longevity or quality of fine clothing. We buy into this kind of marketing hype, because we want to engage in fashion. But somehow we feel that it is special to elevate low-end fashion, while diffusing high-end.

The mass media has an enormous influence on the fashion they would like us to purchase. The constant chasing of trends we don't really need, and wearing facsimiles or "*looks*" of luxury fashion designers has left us feeling lousy with a closet full of clothes, of which their origins are unknown. People do crave connections with things including clothes, that gives us meaning and joy. As Marie Kondo asks her clients; "*Does this...um, really spark joy? I can think of no greater happiness in life than to be surrounded only by the things I love.*" Buying has intensified, in the hopes that we'll find that perfect something.

Lost Skills. Clothing is a basic need, and caring about what we wear should have more meaning than a craving for the latest trend. It's a fact that caring about clothes, obsessing over perfectly stitched seams, matching the textile designs of pattern pieces, and indulging in the hand of a luxurious fabric, develops a relationship with the things we wear and makes us feel proud.

The act of sewing on buttons, attaching a fallen hem, adding patches, or mending a small hole in a favourite sweater helps us gain an appreciation for the design and creation of clothing. These are the common sense know-how skills that we used to learn. One reason these skills are being lost, is that they aren't typically taught in schools as they were in previous decades. Considering how inexpensive clothing is, we think the cost of repairs is not worth the bother and go buy something new. I thought the very same way when I bought a pair of Joe Fresh jeans, and within two weeks the zipper broke; the repair would have cost more than the jeans.

What is fashion now?

If one looks back at the fashion from previous decades and even centuries, popular styles are relatively easy to identify, and are used in the study of costume history. During the 1920s, it was the first time women exposed their legs, so shorter dress styles were popular. One of the most recognizable dress styles of this era is the flapper, often made from lightweight silk chiffon and adorned with beads and fringe. The introduction of the Chanel suit in this same time period, along with Coco Chanel's signature string of pearls were other distinctive styles. From the 1950s and 1960s these stylish women, Audrey Hepburn, Grace Kelly, and Marilyn Monroe remain icons for these classics, such as the LBD (little black dress), the Kelly bag by Hermès, and the fitted black skirt and suit jacket with a peplum waist. All of these items of clothing and accessories mentioned above remain as classics to this day, and are a mainstay of fashion's vocabulary.

With the introduction of fast fashion in the late 1990s, and its tremendous influence at all levels of the ready-to-wear industry, the distinctive styles of fashion that were popular in each of the prior decades are inconspicuous. Because fast fashion manufacturing is based on knock-offs of existing fads and trends, today's fashion consists of a bunch of *"looks"*, rather than characteristic styles. There are no radical changes in terms of details like luxe fabrics or decoration that marked popular fashions in earlier times. I would argue that in North America, the fashion system and the push from media may well have created mass produced individuality. After all, we want to be fashionable, because we attach special status to people who are in fashion. They are admired, envied, and alternatively criticized for the way they look and what their style represents. But it is difficult to be unique, and stand out in a world, where there is so much choice, and pressure to wear clothing, no matter how uncomfortable or unflattering it may be.

The primary goal of the fashion industry is to replace fashions with the latest. Economists will tell you that the more something is subject to rapid change, the demand for cheap products of its kind increases. But as choices keep growing negative aspects of having a multitude of options begin to appear. Ready-to-wear's prevalent linear business model creates a vicious cycle of produce-buy-discard. The highly profitable fast fashion practice of copying designers, making garments in cheap fabrics, with little attention paid to quality and construction, lowers our expectations of clothing. We can't recognize quality fabric and properly constructed clothing, and low price signals that a product is disposable. Why buy better or at a reasonable price, when fashion is in style for only a season? Because dress symbolizes our societal values, all we're saying is that we can discard and replace at our convenience for little money.

Our view of fashionable clothes has undeniably changed. We have closets full of looks, valuing price over quality, which serves us well enough for its short intended use. To see how we can cultivate better strategies towards sustainability, and a greater respect for our clothes, it's time to dig deep into what will help us make much needed change, beginning with the science behind clothing's main ingredient - *fabric*.

Chapter 3

Understanding The Science
Behind Our Clothing

"We no longer bother to mess with our jeans; we'd rather buy a pair that already has someone else's vision imprinted on them." Orsola de Castro

I'm fascinated by the beauty and tactile qualities of textiles, such as silk velvet and woven paisley. I don't know if my fabric obsession is innate, but an education in fashion design and manufacturing, opened my eyes to the world of textiles. Clothing's main ingredient is fabric. The components that make up fabric provide essential information as to how a garment will perform and meet our expectations. Learning about these components and the production processes used to make fabric will help you choose better quality items, properly care for your clothes, and hopefully encourage fashion manufacturers to do a better job at designing and constructing clothing.

Fibres are the basic components or the raw materials of textiles. All fibres are spun into yarns, which are then woven or knitted into fabrics. Fabrics like leather and ultrasuede are referred to as nonwovens or formed textiles. Most of our everyday clothing is made from woven and knitted fabrics. Prior to WWII, fabrics were made entirely of natural fibres such as silk, wool, cotton, and linen. The earliest artificial fibres were rayon and acetate. This chapter discusses the characteristics of the most common fibres and fabrications used in our clothing. There is no perfectly green fabric, and most of the environmental damage occurs during the textile production phases.

Getting to Know Fibres
System of Fibre Classification

Fibres are classified as **natural**, consisting of cellulose (vegetable) and protein (animal) fibres; and **manufactured**, consisting of cellulose-based fibres (cellulosics), synthetics, and metallic fibres. Cellulosics are fibres made from regenerated cellulose, typically wood pulp, and are manufactured by the same processes used to make synthetic fibres. Synthetics are manufactured from artificial materials through chemical synthesis and bear no resemblance to fibres from natural sources. Today, most of the fabrics used in our clothes are blended, or rather combinations of two or more fibre types.

Natural fibres like wool and cotton are already in a form (staple) that is ready for conversion into yarns and fabrics. **Staple** fibres refer to short fibres that resemble natural fibres in length. Almost all of the natural fibres including wool and cotton naturally grow as staple fibres. Manufactured fibres are produced from raw materials and made in long lengths of fibres or **filaments**, which are then cut into short staple lengths before spinning into yarn. The only natural fibre in filament form is silk.

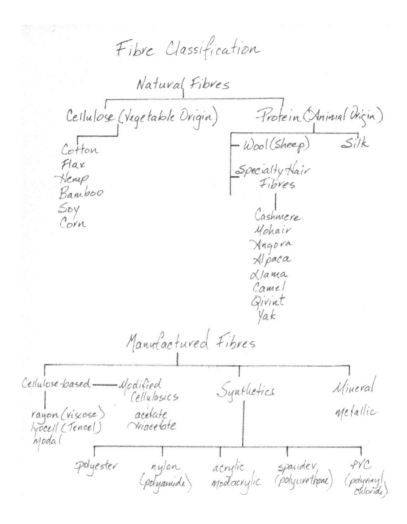

Fibre Classification

Natural Fibres

Cellulose (Vegetable Origin)
- Cotton
- Flax
- Hemp
- Bamboo
- Soy
- Corn

Protein (Animal Origin)
- Wool (Sheep)   Silk
- Specialty Hair Fibres
  - Cashmere
  - Mohair
  - Angora
  - Alpaca
  - Llama
  - Camel
  - Qivint
  - Yak

Manufactured Fibres

Cellulose-based —— Modified Cellulosics
- rayon (viscose)
- lyocell (Tencel)
- Modal

  acetate
  triacetate

Synthetics
- polyester
- nylon (polyamide)
- acrylic modacrylic
- spandex (polyurethane)
- PVC (polyvinyl chloride)

Mineral
- metallic

Fabric's Serviceability

All the components that make up a fabric affect a garment's end use, as well as meeting your expectations, and those of designers and manufacturers. There are concepts used to describe the various properties of fibres and yarns which affect the finished fabric. These include *durability, comfort, aesthetics* or *appearance*, and *care*. All fibres carry unique properties that affect the serviceability of the resulting fabric.

Durability refers to how long a product will last, and is determined by several factors inherent in the types of fibres, yarns and the fabric's structure. The properties of fibres and yarns, including strength, absorbency, and abrasion resistance are key to the longevity of a garment. Strength refers to how much pulling force a fibre or yarn can withstand before breaking. Some fibres are very strong like nylon and resist abrasion. Absorbency is the ability of a fabric to take up moisture. Natural fibres have much higher absorbency rates than synthetics. Abrasion resistance identifies how a fabric responds to friction, like rubbing, which typically occurs around necklines, collars and cuffs. Another important property is resiliency or the ability of a fibre to return to shape following wrinkling. Related to resiliency is dimensional stability, whether or not a fabric can retain its size or shape over time. If a fibre is elastic with good recovery, the resulting fabric is dimensionally stable. On the flip side, if you own a pair of highly elastic socks that don't return to their normal size, they are unwearable.

Absorbency is also important to the comfort of a fabric. The comfort of the body will depend on how fabrics deal with the evaporation of moisture. Athletic gear and activewear are touted as fabrics which "*wick moisture*", allowing the moisture to pass along its surface. Wicking is typically a feature of synthetic fibres because they naturally resist absorption. All of the natural fibres have high absorption rates, rendering them breathable and comfortable to wear.

The subjective term "*hand*" describes the feel of a fabric and affects comfort. Some words used to describe the hand of a fabric include crisp, rough, firm, smooth, soft, fluffy, and silky. Denim fabric without the addition of Lycra or spandex is stiffer and more inflexible, which some individuals find uncomfortable.

Annoying static cling? Static charge or electricity is generated by friction and builds up in fibres, especially those with low absorption rates, creating problems such as clinging, soil retention in the fabric, and shocks. Hydrophobic fibres that absorb very little moisture build up static, a common problem in dry climates. In dry winter climates polyester garments cling because of low moisture in the air. When the air is dry, you can also get static produced in natural fibres that normally absorb moisture, like wool and silk.

The appearance of a fabric is a subjective concept that describes its visual effect on people. No matter how durable or comfortable a product might be, if a customer doesn't like its appearance it won't be worn. Some properties that define a fabric's appearance are colour, the luster or sheen of the fabric surface, drape or how the fabric hangs, and loft, how fluffy or bulky a fabric is. Loft is determined by the air space between the fibres, which provides warmth or insulation.

A propensity to pill, is a characteristic which affects appearance. Pills are the unattractive, fuzzy balls on the surface of sweaters or other textiles. These balls are the result of short fibres entangling on the surface of a textile, caused by abrasion or friction, such as continual rubbing of sleeve elbows. Pilling is undesirable, not only because of its unsightly appearance, but also because it is uncomfortable next to the body. Strong synthetics like nylon and polyester are problematic, because the pills aren't easily removed from the surface. Acrylic knits are very prone to pilling. Pills are rarely seen on collars of cotton shirts, but shirts made of polyester or polyester-cotton blends will pill in this same area.

The care of a textile depends on the fibres used, yarn structure, fabric construction, dying and finishing methods used, and how the item is stored. Shrinkage and stretching are problems that occur during cleaning.

Natural Fibres
My Love Affair With Wool

If I had to choose one fibre I couldn't live without, wool would be it. I began to notice how little wool was in our clothing, while on the hunt for a new suit. I've never contemplated wearing anything but a wool suit. Wool is the number one yarn of choice for knitters, and my drawers are filled with hand-knit wool sweaters that I've had for over ten years, some even as old as twenty.

Wool was the first animal fibre to be woven into fabric. Sadly, wool fibre accounts for less than 1% of the total global fibre market, and has taken a back seat to polyester and cotton production. Together, Australia, New Zealand, and China produce almost half of the world's wool products. Allover the world, there are many small cottage operations making wool yarn and other products, especially for the hand-knitting industry.

Wool is the hair fibre that comes from sheep. The term *"wool"* is often used loosely to describe all yarn, but is also used inaccurately to describe the hair from other animals. True sheep's wool has unique properties different from other animals. If you were to travel the globe, there are far more sheep than any other type of farm animal, and they include an amazing diversity of over 200 breeds. The best quality for textiles comes from breeds such as Merino, which dominates the world's sheep industry. Merino produces a luxurious, fine soft fibre. Other types of wool, including Icelandic breeds produce coarser fibres, which are highly durable and popular for outerwear, like cozy Aran cable sweaters.

Most sheep are sheared twice a year to harvest the fibre, once in the spring and once in the fall. Depending on the breed and the frequency of shearing, the fibre length averages between 2 inches (5cm) for finer wools to 12 inches (30.5cm) for long-wools. The mass of fibre shorn from sheep is referred to as fleece, which contains everything that was on the sheep at the time it was shorn - including vegetable matter, dirt, and lanolin, the natural oil secreted from the sheep's glands. Commercial farmers bundle fleece into bales for shipping to factories. The factories further scour, card, and comb the wool prior to spinning into yarn, and further processing depending on the desired finished product.

Wool is desired for its special properties. It's resilient and elastic, springs back into shape after being stretched, wears well, and resists wrinkles. A pair of wool trousers worn all day, and hung in the closet overnight, the wrinkles miraculously disappear. It has excellent insulating properties due to its natural crimp or wave that traps air.

Wool is different than any other fibre because it is comfortable to wear in both warm and cold climates. This characteristic makes wool one of the best fabrics for outdoor garments and accessories. "*Hygroscopic*" describes this unique property. The outer layer of overlapping wool scales are hydrophobic (repels water), and the interior of the fibre attracts water. Wool absorbs up to one third its weight in water, shedding liquid easily, while allowing garments to maintain their insulating properties, feeling both warm and dry to the skin when wet. I've never been convinced of the hype surrounding the "*wicking*" property of synthetic fibres used in much of our athletic clothing. The moisture can build up, doesn't evaporate very well, and potentially leaves you feeling hot and clammy. Wool stands up far better.

Wool is naturally flame retardant, and a favourite for fire blankets, home décor and industrial fabrics. Wool fibres are self-extinguishing when exposed to flame. The high absorption rate keeps wool from conducting electricity. Wool acts like a magnet to prevent dirt from moving deep into the fabric.

From my experience in the yarn business, wool gets a bad rap from customers unfamiliar with the variety of wool products. The common complaint is being "*allergic*". A true wool allergy is rare, and usually exhibits as a rash on the face, arms, and hands. If you have an allergy to wool, any creams or makeup containing lanolin will cause the same reaction as when exposed to the fibre. Medical experts believe it's the allergen from the alcohols that make up lanolin, the oil in sheep's wool that causes a reaction.

Wool sensitivity is different from a wool allergy. Many people who think they are allergic just have sensitive skin, and are uncomfortable wearing wool. What causes this sensitivity? In answering this question, one has to look at the structure of wool fibres. The surface of a wool fibre is covered with scales that vary in size, and determine the fineness or coarseness of wool. Fine, soft wool has as many as 2000 scales/inch, whereas coarse wool has as few as 700 scales/inch. The larger scales of coarse fibres is what causes skin irritation or an "*itchy feel*". More often, irritation is caused by the dyes and cleaning chemicals used in the manufacture of wool yarns and fabrics.

Have you ever accidentally shrunk a wool sweater? The scales are also responsible for felting, which describes the shrinkage of wool and other animal hairs. The use of felted wool for clothing can be traced back tens of thousands of years. Felting is deliberately achieved through a process that includes heat, moisture, and friction to form a matte fabric, often made into products like hats and melton fabric. When the scales are exposed to heat, agitation and moisture, the fibres entangle forming a dense, matte fabric. The potential for shrinkage is the reason that most wool knits are hand-washed.

Today, there is a special treatment applied to wool to eliminate the scales, which renders the wool fabric machine washable and prevents shrinkage. The term used to describe this type of process is "*superwash wool*". The main drawback of this treatment is the potential to stretch. I have experienced this problem with some superwash hand-knitting yarns, and found that stretching often occurs during machine washing, and the pieces don't easily return to their original size.

The most popular, luxurious, soft wool comes from Merino sheep, and is comfortable next to the skin. Icelandic breeds produce a coarse, scratchy fibre that is highly durable. Both fine and coarse wools have their place in our clothing. Indulge in some wool, and it will reward you for years to come.

Specialty Hair Fibres
Cashmere - An Experience Not to be Missed

Owning a classic cashmere knit garment is a cherished symbol of luxury fashion. You'll never experience such softness melting in your fingers. Cashmere refers to the downy undercoat of hair fibres of the Capra hircus laniger or Kashmir goat. The cashmere down of this animal provides it with insulation against the cold weather, and is three times warmer than wool.

Originally, cashmere was specific to Kashmir, a high valley between two mountain ranges of the Himalayas on the Indian continent between India, Pakistan and China. During the 18th and 19th centuries, the local Kashmiri population spun and wove the undercoat into a fine fabric, which was made into a shawl style known as *"pashmina"*. These shawls were highly valued. A true pashmina shawl is made from cashmere, sometimes blended with a small amount of wool. Today, there are many copies or fake pashminas in the market, which are often made in synthetics like acrylic. China is now the largest producer of cashmere products. Mongolia, Tibet, India and Afghanistan are other sources of cashmere.

The dual coat of the Kashmir goat consists mainly of guard hairs, which are straight and stiff. Beneath the guard hairs grow the extremely soft down called cashmere. These hair fibres are very fine in diameter, with a soft, silky touch, and 30% lighter in weight than wool fibres, providing warmth without the weight. Cashmere fibres have a slight crimp, with lower elasticity than wool, but still have good resilience. Cashmere is a more delicate fibre than wool.

Quality cashmere production is maximized by four important traits: the defining characteristic is the fineness of the fibre, quantity, how the fibre feels and looks, and a clear distinction between the guard hairs and the cashmere. Too many guard hairs present decreases the fabric's quality.

Cashmere fibres are collected in a few different ways. A goat sheds in the spring and summer, releasing large clumps of fibres. In China and Mongolia, the down is usually combed off by hand with a wide tooth comb. This is the best method of collecting a high percentage of pure cashmere with a minimal amount of guard hairs. In some countries, the animals are completely shorn, and dehaired to separate the guard hairs from the cashmere. This process requires skill or the fine cashmere fibres may be damaged. The high price tag is related to how and when the cashmere is harvested, and other production processes. A poor quality cashmere sweater will often have long, stiff fibres or guard hairs projecting from the surface, and the hand is not as soft as the finest cashmere.

Because cashmere is a premium fibre, manufacturers cut costs by adding a small percentage of cashmere blended with other fibres. Quality blends include cashmere and merino wool, cashmere and silk, and cashmere with baby alpaca. These blends are just as luxe as 100% cashmere. Be wary of blends that mix many different natural and synthetic fibres with a small percentage of cashmere. This diminishes the quality and luxury of cashmere, as well as the benefits of pure cashmere.

Mohair - The Fluffy Fibre

Mohair comes from Angora goats, not to be confused with angora from rabbits. The major sources are from Turkey. Some animals are domesticated in South Africa, and in the southwest US. Mohair goats are not hardy animals, and can't survive in northern climates. Mohair goats are cute creatures, with long curly hair reminiscent of a salon perm.

Kid mohair is the hair from the first two shearing of young goats. Young goats typically grow fine, silky, soft fibre, which has the highest commercial value in clothing. The fibre size increases with the age of the goat; a young goat yields fine, silky fibre, and an older goat has thick, coarse fibres that are more often used in carpets and outerwear.

Mohair has most of the wonderful qualities of wool; soil resistance and high moisture absorption without feeling damp and cold. It is warmer and stronger than wool. Its major advantages include, good abrasion resistance, excellent resiliency, and adaptability for the production of durable, complex yarns like bouclé, and fancy weave fabrics.

Mohair is often blended with wool, cashmere, alpaca, silk, or a synthetic to help the fibres cling together. Mohair fabric and knitting yarns have a beautiful soft halo effect. A high percentage of mohair fibre in a fabric may cause shedding, lessening its appeal in clothing.

Angora - Another Fluffy Fibre

This fluffy fibre waxes and wanes in popularity, and in the 1950s was often used in women's sweater sets. It's the least expensive of the luxury fibres, and its warmth rivals that of cashmere, and has the extreme softness of qiviut.

Angora is a very soft, fluffy, and warm fibre that comes from the angora rabbit. Instead of being shorn, high quality angora is combed from the rabbit when the animal naturally sheds. Angora fibre is extremely *"clean"*, that is you'll get almost 99% pure angora right off the animal. In the past, Turkey, England, France and other countries raised angora rabbits for luxury fibres. Since China is now a major manufacturer, combing rabbits has been supplanted by live plucking in more unethical businesses.

Angora fibre is a very short staple with low elasticity, making it difficult to spin. For this reason, manufacturers often combine it with other fibres. It's commonly blended with wool which adds elasticity. Because angora fibres are short, the fabric can shed as much as it does from the animal. If the yarn has been blended and processed properly, the resulting garment sheds less, and wears beautifully. High quality angora creates a lovely halo effect admired in knitwear.

There are other specialty hair fibres that are more commonly used in hand-knitting yarns than in clothing, but have qualities that make luxurious fabrics. These include alpaca and llama, both members of the camel family, camel hair from the Bactrian two humped camel, qiviut from muskox, and yak, native to the high altitude regions of Tibet, Mongolia and South Central Asia.

Silk - The Fibre Wooed For Centuries

Before the advent of fast fashion, I always had a few silk blouses and dresses in my closet. They were beautiful, luxurious pieces that I loved wearing. Today, 100% silk is more difficult to find in clothing, even in high-end collections. A small percentage of silk is usually blended with synthetics or other natural fibres. Silk accounts for less than 1% of the global fibre market. Silk is widely perceived as the most beautiful of all the natural fibres, and no single synthetic comes close to replicating its properties. Silk is the designer's dream fabric.

Legend has it that silk was discovered by a Chinese Empress around 2600 BC, when a cocoon fell from a tree into her tea, extruding its fine filament. Thus were the beginnings of this brilliant fibre that has been wooed, prompted thievery, and created the longest road in China, the ancient trade route between China and Rome. For 3000 years, China held the secret of the silk industry. China is still the leader in silk production, followed by India, Uzbekistan, Brazil, Iran, and Thailand. Cultivation of silk and the manufacture of silk textiles was big business in Italy and France prior to the Industrial Revolution. Italy and France no longer farm silk, but are important manufacturers of silk textiles in the regions of Como and Lyon, respectively.

Today, silk is produced under controlled conditions called sericulture, which is an expensive and labour intensive process that makes it unaffordable at all levels of the market. Because sericulture is mostly a manual process, production is common in countries with low cost labour forces.

A variety of silkworms produce silk. The silk is obtained from the cocoons of their larvae. The most common species of silkworm cultivated in sericulture is the Bombyx mori.

Their larvae eat only mulberry leaves, rendering the fibre a shiny, pure white. Another common silk fibre is Tussah, which comes from a wild or semi-cultivated silkworm. These feed on many different types of leaves, most of which contain tannins that impart colour to the fibre. The resulting fibre ranges in colour from off-white to light brown. Tussah fibres are coarser, with an irregular surface, less lustrous, and stronger than Bombyx mori. Tussah silk is also less expensive.

The cocoons are subjected to heat to unwind the fine, lustrous filament in one continuous strand. Silk is the only natural fibre that produces a filament, rather than staple fibres.

The production of silk creates very little waste, but uses a large amount of energy. The silkworm begins its journey to a filament by indulging on chopped leaves, growing 10,000 times its original size, or the size of a peanut shell. When the worm stops eating, it is ready to spin its cocoon. At this point, the worm secretes a continuous filament of fibroin, a liquid which protects it while in the cocoon. The filament itself is coated with a gummy substance, sericin, which is secreted by the worm's glands to protect the cocoon. Within two or three days, the silkworm will have spun around 1600 metres (5500 feet) of filament encased in its cocoon.

Once the cocoons are complete, the workers have approximately two weeks to gather and "*stifle*" further growth, to prevent the silkworm from metamorphosing into a moth. If a moth works its way out, the filament breaks, lessening the value of silk. A few moths are allowed to hatch, to continue the process.

At this stage, cocoons are soaked in warm, soapy water to degum the sericin coating. A point of contention for activists is the harvesting of live cocoons (chrysalis), which have to be killed to eject the fibre. Silk that doesn't have sericin removed is called raw silk. After a water rinse, the silk filament is reeled and unwound. Reeling is labour intensive, but reeled silk is the finest quality used to make woven fabrics. Spun silk is a second type usually found in hand-knitting yarns.

The silk fibres are cut into shorter lengths, carded and spun. The waste silk from reeling is used to produce spun silk. A third grade is noil silk yarns, which are processed further than spun silk. You may have heard of Duoppioni or dupion silk, a result of two worms that nest together and form one cocoon with a double stranded filament. This is a rare occurrence in nature, so this type of silk is expensive.

Silk is one of the strongest natural fibres. Quality pearl necklaces are strung with silk yarn. It's an excellent insulator to keep you warm. Long silk underwear and silk lined sleeping bags provide unequaled warmth for winter activities. Silk is a poor conductor of electricity making it susceptible to static cling in drier climates. Silk dyes well in bright colours.

Silk is purchased by weight, and the process of degumming causes a loss in weight. Because it's sold by weight, a common practice in the silk industry is "*weighting*" the fabric, or loading it with finishing substances. Weighting is often done in the dyeing stage, and lends the fabric a crisp, firm feel and a lustrous sheen.

Silk has similar moisture absorbing properties as wool, easily absorbing and releasing moisture away from the body. Although silk is a strong fibre, it has other characteristics which make it less durable, and not as versatile as wool. Silk has little elasticity, lower resiliency and flexibility than wool. It has a tendency to stretch with wear, and is slow to recover. After washing silk, it usually goes back to its original shape. Silk tends to fade more readily with each successive cleaning, and over time may develop a fuzzy surface.

An unusual characteristic that you may have experienced, is an odour from wet silk. This odour occurs with Tussah and lower grade silks. The smell sometimes disappears after the first few washings. If silk has not been properly processed, the smell may be strong, indicating a lower quality fibre. For the most part, this is the nature of wet silk.

Pure silk is very smooth and slippery, lacks body, and forms a relaxed, drapey fabric. Because of the expense of producing 100% silk, it's often blended with other fibres. A pure silk textile will last longer than a silk fabric mixed with other fibres.

Natural Cellulose Fibres
Cotton - Once the King of Fibres
There was a time when the advertising tagline "*The Fabric of Our Lives*" described the most widely used fibre in the world - cotton. Cotton was the leading fibre of the global trade market until synthetics, mainly polyester exploded in the early 2000s, coinciding with the introduction of fast fashion. Cotton makes up around 25% of global fibre production, because it is the most practical of all the natural fibres.

Historically, cotton has colonized and controlled world economies, as far back as the ancient civilizations. Since the Industrial Revolution, cotton production has been fraught with exploitive practices. It's still a significant industry in many of these countries, including the Middle East, South America, Africa, the southwest US, China, Australia, Pakistan and India. China, India and the US grow over one half of the world's cotton.

Cellulose fibres occur naturally in plants. Cotton is the soft, downy fibre growing around the seed pod or "*boll*" of the cotton plant. Cotton grows best in warm, humid climates like those in Egypt, India, China, South America, and the southwest US. Cotton is classified according to its fibre or staple length, colour grade, brightness, and fineness. The fibre length is most important to the quality of cotton; the longer the staple as in Pima, Egyptian, and Sea Island cotton, the better the fibre properties. These luxury types of cotton are very soft, and more expensive to purchase.

As well as being able to grow organically, cotton can be genetically engineered to produce coloured fibres without the use of dyes, albeit the colours are soft hues. Since cotton is the most widely produced natural fibre for textiles, and because of conventional cotton's negative environmental effects, it has seen the most growth in organic production. Although organic cotton is better for the environment, it represents a small percentage of world cotton production. Statistics for 2018 from the Textile Exchange show that around 10% of cotton sourced globally was organic. But there was a 56% global growth in organic cotton production in 2017/18, a good sign for continued growth in this type of farming. The next chapter will explore the differences between conventional and organic cotton from an environmental perspective.

Cotton has high strength, and is stronger when wet, making cotton fabrics easy to launder. Dyed cotton retains colour longer if washed in cold water. Generally, cotton has to be treated to prevent shrinkage. Cotton has poor elasticity, and low resiliency with cleaning and wear. Sunlight causes oxidation, turning white cotton fabric yellow. Depending on the quality of cotton, a cotton garment tends to get a worn, fuzzy appearance over time. A wool garment will be enjoyed for many years longer than one made of cotton.

Mercerization is a chemical finish used on cotton that adds luster, giving it a silk-like appearance, and increases its uptake of dye. Mercerized cotton is stronger, less prone to shrinkage than regular cotton, and is more comfortable to wear. Cotton also blends well with other fibres, including wool, linen, rayon, and synthetics.

Linen - The Ultimate Summer Fabric

100% linen fabric is one of my favourite textiles. "*Linen*" is the term that describes fabric made from the stem of the flax plant, a bast fibre. The proper name for the fibre is flax, but linen is commonly used as a generic term to describe flax fibre and woven textiles. Flax is generally considered to be the oldest of the textile fibres, and was extensively used in the ancient civilizations around the Mediterranean, as it made a cool, breathable fabric to wear in the hot climate. Linen fragments have been found in excavations in Switzerland, dating back to around 10,000 BC, and intact remains have been found in Egyptian tombs.

The flax plant is cultivated as a food and fibre crop in cooler regions of the world. Top quality flax is grown in western European countries and in Ukraine. Canada and China are the principal flax producing countries, but Canada is not a significant linen textile manufacturer. Northern Ireland and Belgium are leading exporters of linen cloth.

Flax is commonly known as a sustainable fibre because it requires a minimal amount of pesticides and water, and it even grows in poor soil. Flax plants require a temperate climate, cloudy skies, and adequate moisture. Bright sunlight can damage the plants. The plant grows to a height of 3-4 feet, and is harvested before the seeds are ripe by pulling out the entire plant from the ground. If raised for seeds, these are made into linseed oil. Unfortunately, as with all of the natural fibres, linen represents a small percentage of the global market.

Flax fibres are soft, lustrous, smooth and straight. The harvested bundles look like long, blonde hair prior to processing. Processing of flax is labour intensive, requiring skilled workers. Flax is the strongest of the plant fibres, and like cotton, it is stronger when wet. Linen's absorbency is higher than cotton, and can also withstand very high temperatures, making linen fabric easy to care for. Flax fibres have very low elasticity and resiliency. These properties cause the extreme wrinkling of linen fabric, a property that many consumers find annoying. Flax is often blended with other fibres such as cotton and silk.

Linen is one of the best fabrics for summer clothing because it breathes, feels cool and is comfortable. Linen fabric doesn't pill, and is resistant to stains. The true beauty of linen is that it gets better with successive washings. You can't say that about many textiles. It becomes drapey, soft and supple with age and laundering. If you've never experienced linen bed sheets, you must try this luxe treat.

Bamboo - Fact vs Fiction

Consumers are often duped by misleading claims touting the environmental attributes of bamboo textiles. These products are often promoted as *"eco-friendly"*. The premise that bamboo textiles are green is usually based on the self-sustainable nature of the plant, rather than how it is processed.

Bamboo fibre comes from the pulp of bamboo grass. It is considered sustainable because it is quick growing, and doesn't require irrigation due to its extensive root system. The bamboo plant can be grown without pesticides and fertilizers, and the farms are easily kept organic.

Although the bamboo plant is a relatively sustainable crop, there are concerns surrounding the manufacturing processes used to make bamboo fibres into yarn and textiles. Bamboo fibre is manufactured using two different methods, mechanical or chemical processes. The mechanical process includes crushing the stalks or the woody part of the plant, much like processing flax to form high quality linen. A mushy mass is formed, and then the fibres are combed out and spun into yarn. The resulting strands are typically too coarse for hand-knitting yarns and textiles. Because this method is labour intensive and expensive, very little bamboo is processed mechanically.

The most common way to form bamboo fibre is with the same chemicals and equipment used in the production of rayon or viscose. Rayon is a regenerated cellulose, meaning the manufacturing of it uses *"natural cellulose"*, combined with synthetic processes to make the fibres. The *"viscose process"* is the most common way to form rayon, which includes the use of strong alkalies, followed by multi-phase bleaching.

The cellulose from the bamboo plant replaces the wood pulp used to make regular rayon. Bamboo leaves and shoots are cooked in strong chemicals (sodium hydroxide), then the liquid is forced through a spinneret (a device used to extrude synthetic fibres) into more chemicals which form fine bamboo strands. These are washed and bleached to form rayon yarn, followed by dyeing. The dyed yarns are woven into fabric or made into hand-knitting yarns. Manufacturers are now required to label yarns and textiles made this way as *"bamboo sourced rayon or viscose"* or *"rayon from bamboo"*, rather than *"natural bamboo"*. Most of the clothing and yarn labelled as bamboo is rayon or viscose.

You can understand a consumer's confusion, when they think a textile is natural bamboo, when that is far from the truth. There are technologies now that use less toxic chemicals to produce rayon from bamboo cellulose. The *"lyocell process"* for manufacturing Tencel, is another regenerated cellulose which is modified to use bamboo cellulose.

Bamboo has a soft touch, and silk-like draping quality, but it can elongate or stretch, especially in a knit construction. Stretching is minimized when it is blended with other fibres. The yarns have a sheen like mercerized cotton, and like cotton, it is breathable and highly absorbent. I have found that because of its high absorption rate, fabrics take longer to dry than wet cotton, particularly bamboo blended bath towels. Natural bamboo has anti-microbial properties, but chemical processing destroys this quality.

Hemp Deserves Some Fashion Attention

Hemp is an underrated fibre, long equated with the hippie styles of coarse, shapeless eco-fashions, and its marijuana connection, a strain of hemp Cannabis sativa. Hemp is the name of the soft, durable fibre cultivated from plants of the Cannabis genus with no psychoactive properties. This resilient plant grows easily all over the world. It is naturally insect resistant and requires little maintenance. It has been used for millennia for its fibre, seed, and oil products. Records indicate its use as far back as 2300 BC. After WWII, cotton took over as the favoured cellulose fibre, almost eradicating hemp production globally.

Hemp fibre is processed much like flax, and has similar

properties to linen, including stiffness and lack of elasticity. Like linen textiles, hemp fabric washes easily and grows softer with wear. Newer modifications have improved the properties of hemp, and is lovely blended with wool. Wool provides the necessary elasticity, and a more comfortable wear. Hemp is another example of a natural fibre that deserves to be used more in our clothing for its durability and sustainable nature.

Manufactured Fibres
Cellulose-Based (Cellulosics)
Rayon - Silk's Replacement

Rayon is not a true synthetic, but rather regenerated cellulose or wood pulp, and manufactured by the same processes used for synthetic fibres. In 1910, rayon was first produced commercially in the US by the American Viscose Company, as an inexpensive substitute for silk. It is considered the first manufactured fibre. Using different chemicals and manufacturing techniques, two types of rayon were developed, viscose rayon and cuprammonium (Cupro) rayon, which was introduced in 1926. Cupro is a higher quality, more expensive rayon than viscose rayon, and is made from the cotton linter waste remaining after cotton is ginned. It is favoured in Europe for higher priced clothing lines. Bemberg® is an example of Cupro used primarily as a lining fabric in high quality tailored garments. Bemberg lining is a light weight fabric, that feels like silk. Rayon has become an overused fibre like polyester, and is in much of our clothing.

Viscose and rayon are two words describing the same thing. North American garments tend to use "*rayon*", whereas in Europe "*viscose*" is a more common term. The use of the term viscose comes from the process known as the "*viscose method*" which makes wood pulp into fibres. Viscose is made by chemically dissolving wood pulp, then it is reformed into fibres utilizing similar synthetic manufacturing processes. The manufacture of regular viscose requires a lot of energy and water.

Viscose rayon is a concentrated industry with around 80% of the market controlled by 10 textile giants. One of the largest producers of viscose rayon, is Austria's Lenzing textile company. Most of the wood pulp mills where the cellulose is dissolved are in these countries: Canada, Brazil, and Indonesia. Most of the finished rayon textiles are manufactured in China.

Rayon is a fibre with a soft hand, and drapes like silk. Because of its high absorbency, it is receptive to dye, resulting in a brilliant, lustrous surface. Although it is highly absorbent, it loses strength when wet, and is less able to recover from stress. Historically, rayon was notorious for shrinking and stretching. Over the years, manufacturers have developed better processing techniques to alleviate these problems.

Developed in the 1950s, modal is the first modified version of viscose. Modal is made from the cellulose of beech trees, and has greater strength than viscose when wet. For this reason, modal is also known as *"high wet modulus rayon"*. The Lenzing company makes the best quality modal, and is known for using more eco-friendly processes, than for the modal produced in China. Another trademark of late for the Lenzing company is EcoVero, another cellulose-based viscose fibre which is more sustainable with a lower impact on air and water than generic viscose. EcoVero is certified with the EU Ecolabel for textile products.

Modal is breathable, soft and stretchy. It is durable, machine washable, and dries faster than cotton, rendering modal less likely to feel cold when wet. Modal is often combined with other fibres. My experience with modal is that it pills more readily than cotton, and its surface gets fuzzier quicker. This may be related to the different ways modal is processed.

Lyocell is a newer member of the rayon family. The first commercial production of lyocell in the US was in 1993. Lyocell is produced from the wood pulp of eucalyptus trees, grown specifically for this purpose, or managed forests. The process of making lyocell uses a solvent spinning technique, in which the dissolving agent is recycled, reducing environmental pollutants in the air and water. This is referred to as a closed loop system. The trade name is Tencel by the Lenzing Company. It is more costly to produce lyocell fabric than viscose.

Lyocell fibres are stronger than the other cellulose fibres, with greater abrasion resistance and durability. The fibres are less prone to shrinkage, possess a soft hand with good drape, and are easily washed. Depending on the fabrication lyocell can have a firmer hand than viscose rayon. There is more lyocell in our clothing now than there was in the early 2000s.

Other Modified Cellulosics
Acetate and Triacetate

Both acetate and triacetate aren't used as much in our clothing, as they once were. Acetate used to be highly popular as a lining fabric in garments, but most linings are now made from polyester. Acetate was first produced in 1924 by the Celanese Corporation in the US. Triacetate or the trade name "*Arnel*" was introduced in 1952.

Acetate is composed of cellulose acetate, and is manufactured as for synthetic fibres. Triacetate is made from the same raw materials as acetate, but the process differs slightly.

Both acetate and triacetate have very low strength and are weaker when wet. Both have good elastic recovery and elongation, but if acetate is stretched too far, it won't return to its original shape. Acetate has low resiliency, and doesn't recover well from crushing or wrinkling. They are both heat sensitive, and must be ironed at low temperatures with steam. Triacetate is often heat-set or treated so it is resistant to stretch and shrinkage, making it outstanding in knit fabrics and for permanent pleats. Both have excellent drape and a soft hand, but their low absorption rates build up static charge.

Acetate suffers from an unusual characteristic that you may have experienced. Air pollutants can cause some dyes, mainly disperse dyes, to suffer from *"fume fading"*. Fume fading changes the colour of the fabric, such as blue changing to the colour purple, and brown turning to pink. Acetate fabric also loses strength and develops splits when exposed to sunlight for long periods of time, and with age. This commonly occurs in jacket linings. For these reasons polyester is more widely used as a replacement for acetate lining fabric.

Synthetic Fibres
The Synthetic Elephant in the Room

Synthetic fibres fall under the category of manufactured fibres. We call fibres synthetic because they are a result of the chemical synthesis of raw materials, primarily petrochemicals or fossil fuels. Because they are made in a laboratory, there is nothing natural about synthetics, and should not be confused with natural fibres from plant or animal sources. They may be produced to resemble almost any natural fibre, but their underlying structure and properties are different from natural ones.

I'm going to put it out there, synthetic fibres should have less real estate in our clothes. It's astonishing that polyester is now the number one fibre produced globally. It makes up approximately 65-70% of the market share, and is in almost everything we wear, regardless of the fact that it has a 100% negative effect on the environment.

Polyester alone is found in more than 60% of the garments on retail shelves. Profitable fast fashion companies would not exist without polyester. Synthetic fabrics are easy to produce, and inexpensive, which fits the fast fashion business model built on low price, and the rapid speed at which new products are introduced.

Polyester's Benefits Highly Overrated

Polyester is nothing but a common plastic, derived from the petroleum and oil manufacturing industry. The first commercial production of polyester in the US was by the DuPont

Company in 1953. It has become the most widely used manufactured fibre, exceeding cotton and all other natural and synthetic fibres.

Polyester fibres have very good strength, and do not lose strength when wet. They have very good abrasion resistance, but are highly prone to pilling as with most synthetics. The strength of polyester is not affected by aging, and it takes a long time to decompose, in some cases hundreds of years. Elastic recovery varies according to the strength of polyester, and is generally good to excellent. Polyester fabrics have excellent recovery from creasing and wrinkling.

Polyester has very low absorption, and is almost completely hydrophilic, that is it repels water. This property contributes to the buildup of static charge. You may have noticed that polyester fabrics tend to float on top of the wash water. This property makes polyester fabrics hard to clean, contrary to marketing messages.

Polyester typically has a low level of wicking, but this level can be raised through certain yarns, fabric construction, and finishes that allow the fabric to carry moisture. An example is microfibres, a type of fabrication usually made with polyester, which is found in much of our active and performance wear. Wicking is overrated in these fabrics, as natural fibres fair much better. Unlike natural fibres, synthetics react differently to heat and flame; they melt, producing toxins and causing severe burns.

People love polyester because of its wrinkle-free appearance and easy care. But polyester is *"oleophilic"*; it easily absorbs oily substances, holding the oil and stain within the fabric, making stain removal difficult. Counter to the claims that we should be washing clothing less often, for the latter reasons polyester needs to be cleaned more frequently. Too much fabric softener used in the rinse cycle can also stain polyester fabric.

Another problem is the ability of polyester to hang on to odours. An odour on the fabric may occur when combined with body perspiration, and is hard to remove. Considering that most of our activewear contains polyester makes no sense whatsoever.

Although polyester fabrics can be easily laundered, they are essentially plastic, shedding microfibres or microplastics into the wash water. Fleece fabrications which are usually made from polyester shed the most microplastics.

Today, polyester is commonly found in blended fabrics with wool, cotton, rayon, or linen, as well as in mono-fibre fabric. The percentage of polyester contributes to easy maintenance, strength, durability, abrasion resistance, a wrinkle-free appearance, and shape and size retention. The bad reputation for feeling clammy and maintaining odours began with the uncomfortable leisure suits of the 1970s, which were often made of Fortrel fabric (textured knit polyester), and the retention of perspiration stains in polyester/cotton shirts. For the most part, these poor properties still exist, yet polyester is in so much of our clothing, simply because it's easy to produce and inexpensive. The recycled polyester used in garments today, is primarily sourced from plastic bottles and not from polyester textiles.

Nylon Became The Modern Choice

As with all of the synthetic material used in clothing, nylon is a plastic based material. Nylon is a long chain polyamide manufactured by polymerization. It is the second most commonly used manufactured fibre, and is the generic name for one of the fibres found in the synthetic group "*polyamides*". Sometimes you'll notice the word polyamide on garment labels instead of nylon. There are a variety of nylons produced. Nylon was first developed in 1935 by the DuPont Company. It was introduced prior to WW11 as a silk alternative for hosiery, but also for the production of parachutes.

The major advantage of nylon is its high strength. It is stronger than most natural fibres with excellent abrasion resistance, and has outstanding shape retention. The fibres can be tightly woven, making it a popular choice for windproof garments and rainwear.

Nylon is hydrophobic, with extremely low moisture absorption. Low moisture regain plus poor electrical conductivity causes the accumulation of static charge. Other drawbacks to be aware of, is that nylon stains readily, and is a scavenger for soil and dyes from other items. This means that white nylon will pick up colour and dirt from other items in the washing machine. White nylons should only be washed with whites. White nylon also yellows with age. The soil redeposition problem, causes greyness in coloured nylon. Lightly soiled garments shouldn't be washed with heavily soiled ones, and need to be rinsed well. Pilling is problematic, depending on the fabrication. I've owned wool coats with only 10% nylon content that pill excessively.

Nylon was the first true manufactured synthetic fabric. As a new fabric with easy care qualities, nylon widened the range of choices. Nylon fabrics began to be used in men's shirts, stockings and slips for women. But the popularity of nylon garments with the exception of hosiery, declined because they were uncomfortably warm, and yellowed. Today, polyamide is the primary fabric for bras and tights. A small percentage of nylon is often blended with other fibres for its strength. Nylon dries quickly and is easily washed, but high temperatures may destroy the fabric. As with polyester, recycled nylon is available for use in the manufacture of fabrics.

Acrylic - The Poorly Performing Alternative to Wool

If you're a diehard knitter, you tend to avoid 100% acrylic yarns like the plague, because of their characteristic "*plastic-like*" hand, and crunchy texture. As a stand alone fibre they are no match for wool, or other natural fibres. A knitter would never spend hours making a complex garment that won't hold up over time.

The first production of acrylic was around 1950, and like

polyester and nylon, it is fossil fuel based. Acrylic began as a replacement for wool because it was less expensive and washable. Acrylic was heavily promoted as an easy care option for pullovers and cardigans, but its properties are less than stellar.

Acrylic has only fair strength, and is adequate for a variety of end uses. It becomes 20% weaker when wet and can stretch after washing. It tends to have poorer recovery than many other fibres, but usually goes back to its original shape if properly cared for. Resiliency is good, resists wrinkling, and creases hang out. Because of its very low moisture absorbency, pilling is a huge problem, and it accumulates static.

As with most synthetics, blends are common. Acrylic blended with wool is often found in knits, and has a better feel than 100% acrylic fabrics. The best applications for acrylic are fake fur, and other bulky, textured fabrics. Modacrylic or modified acrylic is often used to make fake fur or pile fabrics, adding better resilience, minimal stretch, and better durability than regular acrylic. I would never pay a high price for a knit sweater made with acrylic yarn; money is wasted on a garment that won't last.

Spandex Revolutionized the Swimwear Industry

Spandex is an elastomeric fibre in the synthetic category. "*Elastane*" is the same as spandex, and a word that is more commonly used in Europe. Elastomeric fibres are characterized by extremely high elongation, at least 200% with excellent recovery. Rubber and synthetic rubber were first developed in the 1930s. These were used to provide support and improve the fit in items such as foundation garments. The first spandex came out in 1959. Spandex is a synthetic polymer and is comprised of approximately 85% polyurethane. Lycra is the trade name for spandex.

The elongation of spandex is anywhere from 500% and up with excellent elastic recovery. It is a light weight fibre, durable, and hydrophobic or low moisture regain. It is sensitive to heat, and the dryer is not recommended. Spandex is expensive, but as little as 1% is needed in fabric to achieve the desired stretch. The principal end uses include swimsuits, foundation garments, hosiery, athletic wear, denim jeans, and it is incorporated into wool suiting fabrics to add comfort. Recently, I came across an unusual use for spandex, in running shoe laces - totally unnecessary.

Faking it With PVC

The majority of PVC in the clothing market is of low quality, marketed as vegan leather, and is nothing more than a problematic plastic. PVC or vinyon is the common name for polyvinyl chloride, a synthetic polymer composed of at least 85% vinyl chloride. It is used to produce fake leather, because it is inexpensive to manufacture. Leather has its environmental issues, but the use of harmful PVC as a leather substitute is not a good solution. There is work being done on developing plastic-free faux leathers, discussed in the following section.

Leather is one of the most durable and long lasting materials, and before we figured out how to weave cloth, humans wore animal skins. Low quality PVC is no match for real leather. As a fabric, it is not breathable and doesn't absorb moisture, and in those fake leather pants, you'll be sweating in no time. PVC yellows with age, and should not be drycleaned with PERC, the most commonly used drycleaning chemical. PERC renders the fabric stiff and unwearable, by turning the fibre crystalline and inflexible. I used to work in a textile science laboratory dealing with consumer complaints, and I'll never forget the time someone *"brought"* in a pair of PVC pants that could stand upright - we knew what happened.

Metallic Fibres

Metallic threads or yarns are the oldest form of manufactured fibres dating back to ancient Persia and Assyria. These early metallic threads were actually filaments of real gold and silver. Today, metallic fibres are made by laminating an aluminum foil roll sandwiched between plastic film. The laminated roll is cut into narrow strips to form metallic yarn. Metallic fibres are primarily used as decorative effects, because they are incredibly stiff and not useable on their own.

New Fibre & Textile Breakthroughs

The formation of textiles is one of the oldest technologies. All steps in textile manufacturing, from the sourcing of fibres, spinning and yarn formation, dyeing, finishing, weaving, knitting or forming fabrics is where most of the damage to the environment occurs. Educating ourselves about newer sustainable materials, and manufacturers improving and designing with better fabrics will go a long way in reducing fashion's carbon footprint. Many of the newer bio-fabrications reduce the number of textile processing steps, which in turn reduces carbon emissions.

There is a growing interest in new sources of fibres and materials to meet the increasing demand for clothing. The raw materials don't need to come from the usual suspects, including oil extraction for synthetics or leather from animals. One group of manufactured fibres made from regenerated natural proteins have been around for awhile including, corn, soya, and milk.

Corn fibres are high in strength, lightweight, and wick moisture away from the skin. Corn is often blended with cotton or wool. The process of producing corn fibre is low-cost, and uses a minimal amount of energy.

Soybean fibre is said to have been harvested in China more than 5000 years ago. Soybean fibres were introduced in the US, and now are harvested under the trademark Soysilk. Soy is often marketed as a green fibre, because the process doesn't pollute, and the by-products are used in animal feed. But soy crops are often non-organic, and genetically modified to enhance production. Fabric from soybean is softer and more durable than cotton, and quick drying. It has high absorbency, breathes well, and its touch mimics silk or cashmere. I've knitted with soy yarn, which has a lovely silky feel and lustrous sheen.

Milk fibre is made from casein protein, the main ingredient of milk, and dates back to the 1930s in the US and Italy. Milk fibres have similar characteristics to wool, but have a more silky texture. I've also worked with milk yarn. Although these fibres have been around for decades, they aren't commonly found in our clothes.

Companies and researchers are beginning to design fabrics from biomaterials which mimic the properties of natural fibres and animal hides. Bio-fabrication is the system for producing textiles from biomaterials. Many are closed-loop systems which are highly efficient and economical. It is possible to manufacture textiles that are almost totally biodegradable. Most of these advances are not to scale, due to the high costs of production, but also because a shift to newer fabrications is a slow transition. The future holds great potential for these biomaterials. Here are some of the newer fibre and textile technologies:

Cupro - vegan alternative to silk made from linter, a by-product of cotton, and is manufactured in a closed loop system. Cupro is not new, but the production of it is more sustainable.

Orange Fibre (2015) - this Italian company makes fibre from citrus waste, which has a silk-like texture.

Bolt Threads - one of their products is a lab grown silk alternative made from yeast and sugar. They also make Mylo leather from mushrooms.

Rose Stems - plant based alternative to silk that is smooth and lustrous. The stems, petals and other waste from rose bushes make a biodegradable cellulose fibre.

Pangaia Company - produces a variety of products including: **C-fibre** made from eucalyptus pulp and seaweed powder. The resulting fibre is soft, silky and is biodegradable in water, landfills, and in composting environments. **Flwrdwn** -biodegradable down made from wild flowers, biopolymer, and aerogel. It is hypoallergenic. **Pangaia Denim** - hemp and organic cotton blend.

Nettle and Hemp Denim - great cotton alternative. Blends Himalayan nettle and organic cotton and hemp. Hemp is four times stronger than conventional cotton. Uses much less water in processing.

Piñatex - created by Dr. Carmen Hijosa, and commercialized in 2016. Company produces cruelty-free leather made from pineapple leaves and stalks with wide application for textiles. One ton of pineapples yields 3 tonnes leaves or waste. It is a clean process, which mechanically makes fibres, and plant-based chemicals are used to finish textiles. Hugo Boss and Nike are clients.

Vegea - Italian Company established in Milan, 2016. Producer of wine leather, made from waste discarded from wine making, seeds, skins, and stalks. Bio-oils are extracted and polymerized in a patented process. At end-of-life, the textile can be recycled into more leather, but polyurethane is used in the steps to form this vegan leather.

Apple - waste used to make leather.

Modern Meadow - laboratory grown leather from yeast.

VitroLabs Inc. - a start-up, makes lab grown leather and fur, having the same qualities of traditional leather. This company is transparent about the process: plant a cell from biopsy of living animal, a harmless procedure; grown with essential nutrients and takes a few weeks; harvest once the growth phase is complete, the hides are tanned through a more simplified tanning process because they only grow what's needed.

10X Beta - product development firm in NYC; created a sneaker from recycled CO_2, converting emissions into a product.

Microfibres - A Confusing Term

The term *"microfibres"* has a couple of definitions. One refers to the fine size of a fibre, often incorrectly used in place of *"microplastics"* that are shed from synthetic fabrics. All fabrics shed microfibres, but not all are microplastics.

The other definition of microfibres are manufactured fibres, which are extremely fine and tightly woven to form a breathable, soft, drapey fabric, with improved wicking. The fibres that can be produced as a microfibre fabric are acrylic, nylon, polyester and rayon. Polyester is used most often. These can also be blended with other natural and synthetic fibres.

Microfibre fabrications are costly to make because of slower weaving speeds necessary to form the dense fabric, and the need for more dye to cover the surface area. These fabrics create a *"look"* of quality, and increase durability. Microfibre fabrics have a broad range of end uses, including tailored suits, lingerie and raincoats.

Fibres to Yarns

Fibres must be made into yarns, before they are woven or knitted into fabrics. Yarn is a continuous strand of textile fibres, filaments, or other material that is in a form suitable for weaving, knitting, or otherwise intertwining to form a fabric.

Yarns are either composed of spun or filament fibres. Spun yarns are made of short lengths of fibre called staple fibres.

Most of the natural fibres are staple fibres. Filament yarns are made of continuous strands of fibre that can be meters long. Silk is the only natural fibre that is a filament.

During manufacturing, synthetic yarns are produced in filament form, extruded from the holes of a device called a spinneret. The holes of the spinneret come in a variety of shapes and sizes producing filaments with different properties. Initially, the extruded filaments are smooth and lustrous, and their properties can then be changed to make different types of yarn. For example, texturizing filaments produces a fluffy yarn which mimics mohair. The filaments are cut into staple or short lengths, before they are spun into yarns.

Spinning the fibres into yarns requires a certain amount of twist so that the fibres adhere to each other. The amount of twist affects a yarn's performance. In general, the longer the individual fibres, the less twist that is needed to hold them together. Because filaments are long and smooth, they do not need to be highly twisted. Spinning is done in textile mills, small cottage industry operations, or by hand.

Yarns are further classified into two categories: simple yarns, and novelty or specialty yarns. Simple yarns consist of: a single ply yarn or a single fibre twisted into one continuous strand; 2 or more singles twisted together into a plied yarn (a 4-ply yarn is 4 single fibres twisted together); and 2 or more plies twisted together into a cord (a 4-2ply cord is 4 groups of 2 plies forming the cord). The number of plies does not dictate the thickness of the yarn strand or weight. Plies affect yarn strength and durability. A tightly twisted 4-ply yarn will wear better than a low twist single ply yarn.

Novelty yarns, like mohair, tweed, and bouclé are created by special spinning, twisting or a combination of these processes.

Clothing is Fabric

The manufacture of fashion is complex and labour intensive. The processing of fibres and yarns used to make fabric is the first stage in the fashion's supply chain. Fibres, which are the short staples or filaments of animal, cellulose, cellulosics, and synthetics must be made into yarns, dyed, and then woven or knit to form fabrics, and finally sewn into clothing. Without going into great detail about all the different types of fabric, weaving or knitting methods, the following is a more general discussion of the textile production steps.

Textile mills are factories that process yarn or fabric into useable textiles. There are different types of mills that manufacture at each stage of the production process.

Yarn Mills. Yarn mills take synthetic or natural materials and make them into useable yarns for weaving, knitting or for use in industrial mills. Yarns are spun and twisted, and occur in a number of different forms including fibres that are twisted, or filaments (long strands) laid together without twist. The thread used to stitch clothing together is considered a special type of yarn. Yarn is also made specifically for machine and hand-knitting.

Weaving or Knitting. Weaving is one of the oldest art forms known. Woven fabric consists of sets of yarn interlaced at right angles in some sequence or pattern. The loom, or the device used to weave fabrics is strung with the lengthwise yarns called "*warp*" threads or yarns. The horizontal yarns or "*weft*" threads are inserted over and under the warp to create patterns. In factory settings, the looms are highly complex, noisy, mechanical machinery. Weaving is also a popular artisanal craft, utilizing a variety of weaving methods and tools.

Woven fabrics consist of many different types of weave patterns including plain weave, twill, and basket weaves, as well as fancy decorative weaves like jacquard.

Hand-knitting is another old art form, and evidence of it is demonstrated by sandal socks preserved in Egyptian tombs from around the 4th century in the Middle East. Today's factories use knitting machines, although there are communities around the world which hand knit garments for designers and other manufacturers.

Knitting is the process of forming a fabric by interlocking loops of a continuous strand of yarn with needles. When you knit by hand, you are making a fabric with yarn and knitting needles. In factory settings, flat bed or circular knitting machines rapidly make knit fabric and textile products. Circular machines make seamless items such as socks and hosiery. The first knitting machine was invented by William Lee in 1589. The circular machine was invented in 1816, and the latch needle used in both types of knitting machines was patented in 1849.

Knit fabrics have different properties than woven fabrics, and are primarily known for their excellent elongation or stretchiness. Its innate stretch provides fabric flexibility for freedom of movement.

Dye Mills or Houses. The number one motivator for a purchase is "*colour*". Dyeing fabric is the application of colour with either natural or synthetic dyes. Dyes are chemical compounds dissolved in water or liquid, so they can penetrate the fibres. Dyes are chosen based on their compatibility with fibres. A dye formula used to colour nylon is different from the one used to colour wool. Each fibre type responds differently to the application of dye. Some fibres like silk and rayon generously soak up colour to create brilliant, lustrous effects.

Dye houses impart colour to fibres, yarns or finished textiles. Natural fibres can be dyed at any point in the textile manufacturing process. Most synthetic fibres used in clothing are coloured in the yarn stage. Finishing processes are done in both dyeing and printing operations.

Printing Mills. The art of printing fabric or applied design is thousands of years old. Early printing techniques used simple colouring from vegetable sources, which have a more temporary effect, and fade over time. Some of the most beautiful printed fabrics like Toile de Jouy achieved notoriety in 18th century France.

Printing mills impart patterns onto finished cloth. There are a variety of printing methods including screen printing, which can be automated or done by hand. You may have tried your hand at batik, tie-dyeing, block printing or other methods of applying designs to fabric.

The prominent characteristic of printed fabric is that the dye doesn't fully penetrate the fabric, leaving one side more pale in colour. Luxurious woven fabrics like true paisley are woven with coloured yarns, giving a different effect than printed fabric; both sides of the fabric are equally coloured. Printed fabrics are less expensive to make than weaving patterns of individual coloured yarns.

Finishing is a basic procedural step in preparing fabrics for use, including techniques such as mercerization of cotton, stone-washing or acid washing of denim, and shrinkage control known as "*sanforized*". The term finishing does not indicate a specific colour for the unfinished fabric. The order in which finishes are applied vary depending on the fibre type, fabrication, and the desired appearance of the fabric. Most finishing processes are performed in the same plant as the dyeing and printing operations.

Apparel Manufacturing. The designer's choice of fabric is at the heart of the creative process. The right choice of fabric is fundamental to good design and the success of a garment. After the design specs are created, the fabric is sent to the garment manufacturer to be turned into clothing. Today, the factory setting for clothing manufacture is highly specialized and task based. For the vast majority of workers who make our clothes in countries with low wages, clothing construction is not about garment design, but completing specific sewing tasks in a series of steps.

Predicting a Fabric's Performance

Fabric selection is key to the creative and commercial viability of a designer's collection. The colour and tactile appeal of fabric are essential to the planning of a design, but there are also intrinsic characteristics of a fabric that determine a garment's success for its chosen function.

The strength of a fabric is determined by the types of yarns used, including its fibre content, the number of plies, amount of twist, whether a yarn is composed of staple or filament yarns, the fabric or thread count (number of yarns per square inch), and the number of interlacements of the yarns in the weave pattern. Generally, filament yarns are stronger than those made of staple fibres. The strength of a fabric increases with plied yarn, higher twist and thread count, and tighter weaves. For example, a loosely woven fabric is going to have less strength and lower durability than a tightly woven fabric.

The structure of the fabric affects abrasion resistance, or the damage inflicted when a fabric is rubbed against itself and other surfaces. Yarns with a tighter twist, a balanced weave, and yarns of similar size are more resistant to abrasion, which minimizes pilling. Low twist yarns, fabrics with long floats (yarns on the backside that pass over 2 or more yarns), and yarns like bouclé are easily snagged.

Wrinkle resistance, shrinkage, and a fabric's potential to stretch are affected by yarns. Smooth, low to medium twist yarns, and tighter weaves have better wrinkle resistance. Low twist yarns and looser weaves are more easily stretched, and more prone to shrink.

The selling price of fabrics is based on manufacturing costs, and demand for the fabric. The fibre content, yarn type, and the kind of fabrication affect the cost to produce. The quality and generic type of fibre affects the cost. Cashmere is more expensive than merino wool, because the process of obtaining the fibres is different. Some synthetics like spandex are more expensive to make than other manufactured fibres.

Cost of the yarns is based on the fibre content and yarn construction. Novelty yarns like bouclé are more expensive to make than a simple yarn. The costs of weaving fabric increases with the time it takes to weave, and the greater number of yarns used. Additional costs are incurred through dyeing, printing, finishing, and sewing techniques.

Denim - The Most Iconic Fabric of Our Time

Who would have thought that a rugged pair of pants in dark blue would evolve into fashionable jeans - a status symbol, transcending all ages and economic classes. Six billion pairs of jeans are produced annually, and the average North American owns seven pairs, and purchases four new ones each year. Jeans are one of the most popular garments ever created.

Denim has its origins in France, *"serge de Nimes"*, a fabric initially conceived in Italy and called *"jean"* or *"jeane"*. 100% denim fabric was a niche textile sold in the 1850s by Levi Strauss in San Francisco. Jacob Davis, a tailor picked up some of this fabric and created the first pair of jeans with a button fly and copper rivets, originally known as *"waist overalls"*. Davis and Strauss went into business together mass producing denim work pants. In 1890, Strauss introduced a new silhouette, Levi 501, and to this day the silhouette hasn't changed.

Historically, blue jeans have embodied multiple layers of meaning from workwear, anti-fashion statements, the cowboy, war heroes, bad boys, bohemians, and personalized designer labels. In the 1940s and 50s, the image of the American Cowboy popularized jeans with suburbia. Music and movie stars like Elvis Presley, Marlon Brando and James Dean wore jeans that connote to the *"bad boy look"*. Jeans weren't as popular with women till later. The hippies of the 1960s, popularized bell bottoms, and jeans became the garment of choice for social activities. In the early 1970s, decorative denim with embroidery or appliqué was the rage. Jeans relatively remained the same style since their inception, until 1970 when New York fashion designers decided to create a variety of jean styles and finishes.

An iconic ad campaign by the controversial Calvin Klein featured a young Brooke Shields wearing his designer jeans circa 1980; *"You want to know what comes between me and my Calvins? Nothing"*; rocketed the sales of jeans. Designer denim continued, evolving into artificially distressed jeans. Jeans are one of the easiest garments to repair, mend or customize, but many people prefer to pay a premium for artificially distressed ones that have been sandblasted, acid washed and ripped.

True classic denim is made of 100% natural cotton. The cotton is either dyed with natural indigo before being spun into yarn, or after the fabric is woven. Natural indigo was initially chosen to hide the dirt from the work environment of labourers and miners. Synthetic indigo was used as early as 1905, and today, natural indigo is rarely used in the mass manufacturing of denim. A special woven technique was utilized to avoid fraying at the outer edges. Classic denim jeans are woven into a thick twill weave, forming a diagonal pattern that resists abrasion and tears, and is quite stiff. The warp threads are dyed blue and the weft left white. The first zipper was incorporated in 1954. The most common colour of topstitching thread is orange to match the original copper rivets.

Before 1970 most jeans were made of stiff denim, and were rarely preshrunk, labelled as *"unsanforized"*. Denim manufacturers didn't prewash to prevent shrinkage until the 1960s. After the fabric is dyed and woven it is referred to as raw denim. It may be sold in this form, but typically goes through other finishes and distressing techniques to soften, and then is cut and sewn into jeans and other denim products.

There are many different styles of modern jeans, and now some manufacturers are blending polyester with the cotton to reduce costs. Spandex is also incorporated for comfort and flexibility.

Controversial Leather

Before we figured out how to weave cloth, humans wore animal skins, and over time evolved into the manufacture of a variety of leather goods. Most of leather's environmental effects occur during the tanning process. Leather goods are primarily a by-product of the beef industry, as cowhide is most commonly utilized in leather manufacturing. Other animals used include goat, pig, lamb, and the rare crocodile or alligator crafted into luxury products. Hermès Birkin and Kelly bags made in crocodile or alligator, are only available custom-made by artisans, and retail upwards from $19,000.

The largest hide producers are in Brazil, US, and China. China manufactures the largest amount of finished leather goods, followed by Italy, India, and Brazil. Regardless of leather's manufacturing ills, quality leather goods only improve with age and wear, and are highly durable. That can't be said for most textiles. It's rather easy to upcycle and purchase vintage leather products, keeping them in circulation for a long time. Fake PVC leather is no match for the real thing. Leather is controversial for a variety of reasons, but is a product that should never be considered disposable. High quality leather will be in your wardrobe for years, even decades.

Fur...rr Oui ou Non?

The fur trade was the backbone of the Canadian economy and the sole business of the iconic Hudson's Bay Company, for much of its existence. Hudson's Bay Co. became a crown corporation in 1670. The pelts of animals were the perfect choice for outerwear to protect humans from the freezing temperatures of Canada's northern climate. My father was a bush pilot in the Arctic, and my mother was gifted two muskrat fur coats, one long and one short, which were handmade by Eskimos (Inuit) during the 1950s. They were beautiful, without the use of dyes, leaving the natural colour of the animal. They were so exquisite and durable that they were in her wardrobe until the early 2000s. I'm not anti-fur, but I don't possess any great desire to own fur. In a warming climate, it's not practical enough to justify the cost and care of a high quality fur garment. It is difficult to make a case for needing fur.

The case against fur has raged for decades, and more so than leather, leading to many luxury houses discontinuing fur in their collections. The fur industry promotes fur as natural, sustainable, and ethical. Having studied this industry, there is a lot of truth to this claim, and many northern trappers' livelihoods have been destroyed by activists who don't understand the culture. No one understands the environment more than indigenous trappers.

If you choose quality fur, it's critical to avoid cheap fur; real fur is expensive. The source of the fur should be from companies that treat animals humanely, and the hides should be a by-product, where the animal has been used for other purposes. Approximately 80% of fur used in the industry is factory farmed.

By adhering to correct maintenance, along with proper storage methods in hot, humid summer months, fur is incredibly long lasting. Although costly, fur coats can be remodelled to suit your needs, and make great vintage finds or secondhand purchases. I've seen how fur products are made in a local furrier, and the process involves precise cutting, matching of pelts, and skilled stitchery.

If you have the money, and you're not anti-fur, it is by far a better investment than fake fur. Faux fur tends to be sold as an ethical alternative, but it is far from the truth. Fake fur is a less scrutinized industry, and the raw materials are often sourced from fossil fuels, which inevitably end up as landfilled waste.

Ultrasuede Makes a Comeback
The fabric ultrasuede is a nonwoven fabric, a textile structure made by interlocking or bonding fibres. End uses of nonwovens are common in industrial applications, such as

household and health care products, and popular for automobile upholstery. Ultrasuede was introduced in the late 1960s, and appeared in high fashion apparel. If you grew up in the 1970s, you might remember the popularity of men's ultrasuede sports jackets, and skirts for women.

Ultrasuede is the invention of a Japanese scientist working for Toray Industries, which is still one of the major producers of ultrasuede under the trademark Ecsaine. The information on its construction is limited to patent literature, and the Japanese were quite sensitive about it.

Ultrasuede is a specially formed fabric, and the lighter version is called *"facile"*. The production steps are not exactly environmentally friendly, as the original contained polyester and nylon fibres, impregnated with polyurethane. Toray Industries now makes more sustainable versions, incorporating recycled polyester and plant-based polymers.

Unlike real suede, ultrasuede is washable. Drycleaning is not recommended, as it can lose body and shape. Garments are best lined to keep their shape, and maintain their durability. It is an expensive fabric to purchase. Because of the high content of synthetic fibres, pilling is often a problem, particularly around necklines and cuffs.

How do you know what's in your clothing?

Most countries around the world which manufacture clothing for retail have textile labelling legislation, that impose standards for textile products. All garments must have fibre content labels, as well as care labels. Imagine how much frustration would be caused by not knowing the fibre content or if a textile is washable.

In Canada, no dealer can sell, import or advertise textiles without indicating the fibre content of the textile product, and the manufacturer in both English and French. Manufacturers must also include a textile number. The fibre content of all component parts, such as lining fabric must also be given.

50% cotton, 50% rayon
50% coton, 50% rayonne
Made in Canada
Fabrique au Canada
CA 01220

Since 2000, it has been a law that all garments sold in Canada must have care labels affixed. The labels must be placed in a reasonably conspicuous area, and must remain legible for a minimum of 10 cleanings, or throughout the life of the textile, whichever is less. I'll discuss care labels in more detail in a later chapter.

Clothing is made of fabric, and the basic components of woven and knit fabrics consist of natural or synthetic fibres, blended fibres, and more recently biotech fibres, and recycled materials. Fibres play the largest role in determining how a fabric performs. The variety of yarn types and the way a fabric is constructed also affects its function, and how long a textile will last.

Natural fibres like wool and cotton are already in a form that is ready for conversion into yarns and fabrics. Cellulosics and synthetic fibres are produced from raw materials, and most are spun from chemical polymer solutions. All fibres carry unique properties that affect the serviceability of the resulting fabric. Natural fibres have long been the favoured choice for clothing. Overall natural fibres perform better than synthetics, but unfortunately have taken a back seat to synthetics in the global market. Polyester has become the number one fibre of choice by manufacturers, mainly because of its cost advantages.

We all need accurate information about the raw materials in our clothing, so we can make better choices, but this is only part of the equation. Each fibre and fabric choice has trade-offs, making sustainable sourcing no easy task. Garment labelling has its limitations, providing us with only half a picture as to what goes into our clothing. It's time to dig deep into the environmental and human costs, caused by the production of textiles and garment manufacturing. Fashion has a dark past, but its negative relationship with the environment and humans is even more pronounced in the 21st century.

Chapter 4

Fashion's Footprint

"Volume - that word.
Volume is what gave birth to sweatshops.
Volume is what makes fast fashion so profitable.
Volume is what's stuffing our closets.
Volume is what's rotting in our landfills."
Dana Thomas, Fashionopolis

There is a statistic floating around the internet, that states, *"fashion accounts for 10% of global CO_2 output, more than international flights and shipping combined"*. The fashion industry is a global, complex, opaque supply chain, involving many actors. Because of this industry's complexity, and lack of transparency means we can only estimate its carbon impact. A variety of estimates on global emissions are wide ranging, anywhere between 4 and 10%, and not much is based on science. Fashion's lack of transparency makes it difficult for researchers to collect quality data, which would provide the knowledge necessary to understand the depth of this industry's effects on the environment. And without transparency, it is hard for consumers to make informed choices. Academics tend to shy away from studying the garment industry because of the perceived frivolous nature of fashion. Regardless, the precise negative impact of the fashion industry is unknown, but is sizeable. There is no question that in its entirety the fashion industry is contributing to our climate crisis. This is evident by excess production, environmental disasters of both land and human capital, and the mountains of clothing waste wreaking havoc across the globe.

Most of the environmental damage occurs during the textile production processes in converting raw materials or fibres which are grown, harvested or mined to form fabric, the main ingredient in our clothing. Each step along fashion's supply chain generates potential environmental, occupational, and health hazards. What are fashion's most negligent practices?

Mass Production on Steroids

Since the 1980s, most Western fashion brands have moved from onshore to offshore production. Countries chosen for manufacturing were based on lower wage costs, weaker labour movements, and laxer environmental regulations. Globalization made it possible to produce clothing at increasingly lower prices. By the year 2000, when fast fashion's linear business model entrenched itself, the number of garments produced each year grossly increased. The fashion system is premised on growth, and brands tend not to push for better quality products - just different, cheaper, and faster.

There was a time when designers and manufacturers produced two or three collections a year, coinciding with seasonal changes. Now, fast fashion companies pump out styles weekly, and in the case of ultra-fast fashion, like China's Shein online business, new styles appear daily. Shorter lead times enabled by technology, and revised business systems have led to the production of more frequent clothing lines. Overproduction by manufacturers is a result of the pressure to increase sales.

The acceleration and proliferation of newness is meant to entice customers to continually buy. Customers are nudged through social media and retailers, to constantly satisfy the need to wear new clothes. Fast fashion companies are not the only culprits; luxury houses participate as well - *"fast luxury"*. At one time, the luxury market was based on scarcity, but now they produce excess to satisfy the belief that everyone deserves a piece of luxury. As a consequence, our perception of what clothing should cost, and how much of it we need has shifted. And most concerning, once fashion has no longer served its purpose, it gets thrown into the trash. Overproduction fuels disposability, and today, the pace of production far exceeds the demand for clothing.

Fashion's Addiction to Plastic

Polyester, nylon, acrylic and PVC are the common synthetic fibres used in our clothing, and they are plastics sourced from crude oil. Fabrics made from these fibres create significant problems for people and the environment throughout their lifecycle. They are energy intensive at extraction emitting large amounts of CO_2, and releasing profuse amounts of microplastics during washing or cleaning. Once made, they are difficult to manage as only a tiny proportion can be recycled, and at the end of life they are landfilled or incinerated. Increasingly, synthetics are affecting the health of humans and animals.

Since 2000, we've seen an explosive growth in synthetics. Some experts indicate that the use of fossil fuels in clothing is projected to grow in the next two decades, a driver of net growth in the demand for oil over transportation needs. Synthetic fabrics is a big part of business for oil and gas companies. The top synthetic produced globally is polyester, which has overtaken cotton as the world's most used fibre. Fast fashion companies are awash in virgin polyester, which keeps production costs low, but the environmental costs high. Why?

Polyester encourages overproduction of fashion and waste by-products. Synthetics are readily available, inexpensive, and reliable. You don't have the unpredictable weather and natural disasters that affect crops like cotton, so they are easy to get hold of and manufacture.

The raw materials of polyester are fossil fuels or nonrenewable resources. There are different chemical formulas for the varieties of polyester, but the common one used is *"polyethylene terephthalate"* or PET. This synthetic polymer is molded plastic, formed into polyester filament fibres, which are further blended with other harmful compounds, dyed and finished. The new polyester blouse you bought because you wanted it, came with other potentially harmful additives you didn't ask for.

Contrary to what marketers want you to believe, as of yet polyester textiles can't be recycled. The minimal amount that is recycled, comes with a high price tag. Polyester made from PET plastic bottles has had some success, but remains a niche product. The major problem preventing recycling is the prevalence of blended fibres in our clothing, mixing polyester with other fibres. The technology to separate the fibres is in its infancy, and far from a global system that can collect and properly sort textiles. Most poly-blended scraps end-up in the landfill.

Polyester isn't biodegradable; natural fibres biodegrade much faster. Synthetics are almost *"inert"* and will outlast us. But regardless of any fibre's ability to biodegrade, decomposing fabrics have toxic effects, from the polyester thread used to stitch together garments, plastic buttons, metals, dyes and finishes. We must not think of clothing as whether or not it biodegrades, but that it is designed to be worn.

Polyester fabrics shed toxic microfibres as microplastics, which are released into the water, affecting the health of humans and animals. How a polyester textile is constructed affects the rate of shedding. A smooth polyester fabric sheds less than a pile fabric such as fleece or fake fur.

As we learned in the previous chapter, polyester holds odours, stains readily, and can be uncomfortable in athletic wear, particularly for women. It seems ironic that most athletic leisure brands extensively use synthetics.

The synthetic dyes or disperse dyes applied to polyester, and other toxic chemicals used in finishing fabrics have been shown to cause contact dermatitis and other health problems in humans. 100% cotton or silk fabrics seldom cause reactions in humans.

Many of us are trying to lessen our use of plastic, and some countries in Europe and areas in North America have banned single-use plastics. There appears to be an awareness of the scale of plastic pollution, but somehow we don't think about the amount of plastic in our clothes, likely because of a lack of knowledge and little choice in the marketplace. Brands have done a great job at setting up a situation where the customer believes synthetics are far better than natural fibres. Promotional ads like this one *"Did you know 70% of your clothes are synthetic? Woolite takes care of all types of....."* do nothing but make you believe that this fact is a good thing.

Fibre Exploitation

Before we try to fix fashion's damaging relationship with the environment we need to realize that we can't continue to overuse one fibre above all others. This is exactly what happened with cotton, and now with polyester and rayon. At least to some degree, we can change how cotton is grown and harvested, compared to the extraction of fossil fuels used for virgin polyester, or the chemicals and energy needed to process rayon.

Conventional Cotton vs Organic Cotton

Before polyester jumped the queue as the worlds's most used fibre, cotton was king. Cotton was once the most widely used natural fibre in textiles, but has been bumped to second place. Because of conventional cotton's environmental impact, it has seen the most growth in organic production. Although organic cotton is better for the environment, it represents a small percentage of the world's cotton production. The world saw a 56% increase in the growth of organic cotton in 2017/18, a promising sign for continued growth in organic cotton farms. Because cotton is a major industry to the economies of China, India, and the US, it is important to understand the differences between conventional cotton and organic cotton.

Conventional Cotton

- GMO modified seeds are used to build resistance to bugs
  .
- It often requires pesticides, herbicides and fertilizers (petroleum based), which disturb the ecological balance of the soil, and can contribute to greenhouse gas emissions. Pesticides used to control weeds in cotton fields account for more than 25% of all those used in farming. These chemicals impact the health of farmers and workers, and can cause serious diseases.

- It tends to be grown repeatedly in the same soil, degrading soil quality. Conventional cotton is often heavily irrigated, resulting in water wastage and the removal of important nutrients required for healthy crops. It is a bit of a myth that cotton is a *"thirsty"* crop. Cotton is actually a desert crop with a deep root system, and uses less water than rice, soybeans, maize, and other vegetable crops. The key sustainability issues are typically with management practices, water depletion (irrigated cotton) and water pollution. These issues are dictated by geographic-specific circumstances, such as access to water, mindset, and access to technology.

- Heavy metals, chlorine and chemicals used to dye cotton are toxic. There is potential for chemical residue to remain in a manufactured product after washing, which may lead to skin rashes.

- Machine picking of cotton is common, which can affect the purity of fibres. Fibre waste, breakage of long staples, and loss, reduces the quality of cotton.

- Conventional cotton production leaves a human footprint. The challenges of cotton farming include poor working conditions, child labour, forced labour, health issues, low incomes for farmers, and gender inequality, which holds back community development.

Organic Cotton
- No pesticides required. Insects are used to control pests, so there is little contamination of water sources. Weeding is done by hand, hoeing, or other cultivation processes.

- Crops are rotated. Organic cotton requires less irrigation, reducing water wastage and protects the eco-system. Using better regenerative practices like crop rotation and composting restores soil, and sequestrates carbon from the atmosphere.

- It uses safer alternatives to chemical dyes and whiteners, including natural and water based dyes, and hydrogen peroxide for whitening. No residual finishes are left in products, which is better for the skin and hypoallergenic. Some cotton has been genetically engineered to produce a range of soft colours.

- It uses natural seeds.

- It is usually softer because the cotton fibres are hand-picked. This maintains fibre quality, improves durability and longevity.

- Safer environments for farmers and workers. Cotton farmed sustainably can give farmers and workers decent incomes and improve livelihoods.

- Organic cotton has many benefits over conventional cotton, not only to farms, but also to biodiversity, and much lower greenhouse gas emissions.

Rayon's Impact

Because its properties mimic those of silk, rayon is another fibre that is in too much of our clothing. Rayon is considered one of the first multi-national corporate enterprises, and was big business by the late 1920s. The environmental impact of rayon often goes under the radar, essentially because it comes from many different types of trees including eucalyptus, bamboo, and beech trees, hence its "*natural*" connotation. The most serious consequence of rayon is in the way the raw materials are processed. The wood pulp is chemically dissolved in highly toxic chemicals, and the process of forming this mixture into fibres, requires large amounts of energy. The major effects of rayon manufacturing comes from the use of chemicals, carbon disulphide emissions, deforestation, and the pollution of air, soil and waterways. The development of lyocell, processed in a closed loop system is less damaging to the environment, as are the newer modifications of modal.

Even animal fibres can pose problems for the environment, from unethical practices to the inability to grow crops on land inhabited by grazing animals. Fibres from these sources are nowhere near as problematic as the consequences of conventional cotton, the manufacture of synthetics, viscose processes, or deforestation. Fashion brands moved to exploiting synthetic fibres, primarily polyester and cellulose-based rayon, after having exploited cotton for centuries.

Textile Manufacturing Processes - From Fibre to Fabric

Fashion's largest emissions of greenhouse gases, and other environmental effects happens during the material phases of the supply chain. The sourcing of raw materials are grown, harvested or mined - conventional cotton laden with pesticides is picked, wood cellulose is pulped and bleached with solvents, and crude oil is extracted for the manufacture of synthetics. The next phases include spinning fibres into yarns, dyeing, weaving or knitting, and finishing to form fabric. Fabrics are then cut and sewn into garments, usually constructed by people in low wage countries, often working in less than optimal conditions. Finally, delivery and shipping to retailers and customers also pose environmental problems.

The single worst contributor to climate change happens in the dyeing and finishing processes; the processes by which colour and other chemicals are applied to fabric. Finishing is often performed before dyeing, with some finishes requiring many water rinses, which release toxic substances into the water. These chemicals contribute to over 20% of pollution in rivers and waterways. Water pollution is a major problem in countries like China, Bangladesh, Thailand and Indonesia. Factories performing these processes are also dangerous work environments with potential health risks. Some of the most concerning dyeing or finishing processes occur in the production of denim fashions, and leather goods.

Artificially Distressed Denim

Those coveted jeans in your closet, although originally designed to be durable and affordable, are now artificially distressed, and finished in potentially dangerous conditions with environmental and health consequences. Luxury retailers sell distressed denim at ridiculously high prices, and fast fashion retailers sell similarly made denim at ridiculously low prices.

One of the most harmful methods used to distress denim is *"sandblasting"*. Sand particles are blasted onto denim with a machine, and unprotected workers are at risk for developing silicosis, a deadly respiratory disease. Although sandblasting was banned in Europe in 1966, it is still unregulated and practiced in many countries with questionable safety practices.

The more common processes for distressing denim to look worn and faded include stone-washing, acid-washing and cellulase. Abrasion of fabric is achieved by stone-washing, a mass production laundering procedure that uses lightweight, porous pumice stone. Acid-washing is a bleaching process that consists of soaking or dampening the pumice with oxidizing bleach (sodium hypochlorite); a misnomer since no "*acid*" is used. Dictated by fashion trends, this procedure is also known as frosting or ice washing, providing varying degrees of intensity.

The enzyme cellulase is sometimes added to the pumice, with or without bleach, or used on its own. Cellulase weakens cellulose fibre. The effect on the denim is lightening of indigo dye, but also destroys the fibre "*fuzz*" on the surface. The process has to be properly controlled, so there is minimal effect on the durability of denim. It may seem a mad practice, to deliberately destroy an incredibly durable fabric for the sake of fashion, but there are also the risks taken to human health, and the toxic chemicals that end up in the water.

The Tanning of Leather

The leather industry is highly regulated, but there are many exceptions. Leather processes affect the health of workers, the safety of animals, and leaves toxic waste in waterways. Factories are usually in developing economies, particularly in Bangladesh, where the leather industry is for the most part unregulated. Since leather is a by-product of the meat industry from highly industrialized agriculture, land degradation is also a concern. The leather industry consumes resources and produces pollutants. The authors of "*Cradle-to-Cradle*" describe a conventional leather shoe as a "*monstrous hybrid*" containing a mixture of materials, both technical and biological, and neither can be salvaged after its lifecycle ends. Conventional rubber shoe soles contain lead and plastics. The manufacture of footwear and accessories make up a sizeable proportion of the leather industry.

Depending on the chemicals chosen, tanning leather is the most toxic phase of leather processing. Historically, leather hides were tanned individually by hand with natural ingredients. The word "*tanning*" comes from the use of tannin derived from the bark of specific trees. Leather tanning procedures are divided into different groups: vegetable, chrome, chrome-free or aldehyde, and zeolite based tanning.

Vegetable tanning is the oldest tanning method, using extracts from wood, nuts, trees and shrubs, that can be sustainably sourced. When shoes are tanned with vegetable chemicals, they are relatively safe practices, and the waste from the process poses few problems.

Around 75-80% of the leather items made today are chrome tanned using trivalent chromium III, and in this form is nontoxic to humans. The carcinogenic chromium IV has been phased out in most tanneries. But if chromium III is not properly managed, the toxic form of oxidized chrome is produced and pollutes waterways.

Chrome-free tanning is usually used for specialized performance leather, such as in the automotive industry. The process uses glutaraldehyde. A newer process uses zeolites, a property that regulates absorption and release of water. Water absorption is important to leather's comfort. This procedure is chrome-free, aldehyde-free, and heavy metal free, and doesn't compromise leather's performance. Zeolite based tanning is considered sustainable.

Leather items should not be thought of as disposable, and if designed thoughtfully, constructed well, and cared for, can be lifetime products.

Fashion's Waste Crisis

An unprecedented amount of clothing and textile waste is the by-product of excess production and consumption of fashion products. Fashion in and of itself may seem frivolous, but clothing is not. Most societies wear clothing, at least for protection from the elements. I never thought much about where my clothing ends up. But standing in a textile sorting facility surrounded by mountains of green bags filled with castoffs, I realized the magnitude of our consumption habit.

All consumer products since the inception of mass production are planned with the intent that they need to be replaced with new ones on a regular basis. Planned obsolescence or deliberately designing products to have a short life is a structural issue in western society. Fashion clothing takes the lead in planned obsolescence of consumer products.

Inherent in the word "*fashion*" is change, or the desire for newness. Clothes eventually wear out, but they also go in and out of fashion. Today, even before a product's life is up, the speed with which new products enter the market, and our desire for newness contribute to planned obsolescence.

In Canada, as in most areas of the world, textile waste is the fastest growing category of waste, mostly because of the increased sales of cheap clothing. The belief that clothes are disposable is perpetuated by the continual flood of trends, low prices, poor quality, and our wearing habits. Now the usage phase for clothes is so short, that the vast majority of our clothing ends up in the trash long before their useful life is over. The landfill is typically the most common endpoint of a garment's fate; 85% of textile waste ends up here. In the landfill environment the slowly decomposing textiles release methane gas, which is more potent than CO_2.

Some textiles totally breakdown, but most don't. This is because much of our clothing even if made with natural, biodegradable materials are stitched with polyester thread, and consist of other synthetic and metal components. Natural fibres are biodegradable, but when you factor in all the processing, dyeing and finishing, they still release toxic materials into the soil, as well as releasing methane gas. Our clothing was not meant to end up buried in a landfill or incinerated.

Consider these rates of decomposition: a linen shirt decomposes in 2 weeks, nylon tights in 30-40 years, a polyester dress in 200 years, and your spandex sportswear in 20-200 years. Synthetics are almost inert and take hundreds of years to degrade in a landfill, and during their lifetime expose the environment to a toxic slew of chemicals and microplastics.

Types of Waste in the Supply Chain

There are two categories of textile waste in the supply chain. **Pre-consumer waste** which consists of fabric waste such as offcuts, damaged rolls, solid fibre and yarn waste; and clothing waste including defective runs, cancelled orders, and post-production surplus. The modern fashion industry practice of offering continual discounted prices doesn't ensure that all products will be sold, and inevitably there is a surplus that needs to be dealt with.

The alarming practice of destroying unsold fashion goods and fabrics exists today. Unsold luxury and high-end designer goods, as well as less expensive goods are burned, destroyed or tossed into landfills. Chanel and Louis Vuitton are two of many companies cited in the past for burning unsold merchandise. Around 2018, Burberry incinerated £28.6 million of unsold merchandise, which caused people to take notice. Companies would rather destroy unsold goods than attempt to donate, because they don't want their goods ending up in a discount bin or on the backs of homeless for fear of tarnishing a brand's image.

Historically, textile mills and factories dealt with remnants and reused old stock, which they considered essential system practices. Mechanical recycling, one such strategy has almost disappeared in the fashion industry. Fibres and scraps of cotton and wool can be re-spun into new fibres for yarns and other products. Knitters are able to purchase hand-knitting yarns containing wool, cashmere, or cotton waste sourced from mills.

Post-consumer waste is the by-product of overconsumption. Consumers have become hooked on constantly shopping for new, trendy products at discounted prices. 75% of apparel purchases are at discounted prices. Most traditional retailers compound the problem, because they often own discount outlets, in addition to their full-price stores. We're hooked on cheap, which inevitably ends in excess. We are also duped into thinking that clothes aren't bad for the environment because they can be donated, reused, or recycled.

It feels good to donate unwanted clothing in your closet to charity, but the reality is that there is far more unwanted clothes than people in need. Today, we give without thought, rather than a true act of goodwill. In earlier times, we knew exactly where the surplus went, donating sparingly and carefully.

Not only is textile waste a result of people tossing clothes directly into the trash, but there are also piles of waste left over from what thrift stores and charities can't sell. According to a CBC Marketplace investigation, 200,000 pounds of textile waste is collected every two weeks in the Toronto area. Charities sell approximately 10-30% of donated clothes in their stores. They are also seeing an increase in poor quality clothing that nobody wants. Just as the consumer's closet is brimming, charities are filled with too much cheap clothing that devalues the secondhand clothing business. Good picks are becoming few and far between.

After the good stuff is plucked out, most of the unwanted clothing given to charity is baled and sold overseas to third world countries. Kenya purchases approximately 22 million dollars worth of used clothing a year. These clothes are sold in local markets. Contrary to what we might think, their shoppers are also interested in high quality, fashion forward stuff. What doesn't sell is dumped or burned, the cheapest option. Africa is increasingly seeing poor quality, shoddy clothing. Parts of West Africa now ban secondhand clothing, because these items have had a detrimental effect on local textile manufacturing, an industry with a long history important to their economies. Chile also has a well-established secondhand clothing business, which accepts large amounts of the world's unwanted garments. But more than half of the 60,000 tonnes of textiles imported each year ends up illegally in desert landfills, like one of the largest, Chile's Atacama Desert.

A small percentage of textile waste from donations goes to textile sorting companies that downcycle waste into lower quality products such as insulation materials and rags. Only 1% of unwanted garments or other textiles can successfully be recycled or broken down to make new fibres and clothes.

The Human Cost

Fashion's history has many dirty secrets, none more concerning than its ethics. The industry hides behind its luxe image while exploiting those who make our clothes. And without these skilled workers, fashion businesses would not exist. Apparel production is one of the oldest and largest global export industries. Making textiles and clothing is labour intensive, and as an industry dependent on human labour; no machine or robot can match human hands at a sewing machine.

Globally, the ill effects of the fashion industry on workers have been well-documented. In 2013, fashion's greatest tragedy occurred, with the largest death toll ever at 1133. It happened in Dhaka, Bangladesh, with the collapse of Rana Plaza, a structurally unsafe building housing a number of clothing factories. Workers knew it was a matter of time, before something horrible would happen. Bangladesh's garment industry represents approximately 80% of exports, second largest next to China, but has a long list of factory tragedies.

In the name of efficiency, the globalization of clothing manufacturing has intensified the struggles of garment workers. From the beginnings of factory style clothing production, poor working conditions have caused both industrial tragedies and human struggle. The exploitation of garment workers continues today, and shockingly some manufacturers engage in child and forced labour. The fashion industry is very adept at hiding behind its glamorous facade, making huge profits off the backs of workers, while showing very little social responsibility. From fast fashion to luxury clothing, a brand's image overrides anything nefarious going on.

After the Rana Plaza tragedy, budget brands received the most criticism, but luxury brands flew under the radar because of their prestigious image.

Consumers also have low expectations and standards when it comes to those who make our clothing. We are so hooked on cheap, that we believe that clothing can be made at such absurdly low prices. Consumers are so convinced that inexpensive fashion deals are of value and fair, that they often view with suspicion designers who make quality goods at expensive prices. To be fair, without transparency in the industry, it is hard to make informed choices, when fed misinformation or none at all.

Globalization and the single-minded pursuit of cost advantages by large fashion corporations, results in exploitation; people are not compensated for the full value of their labour or acknowledged for their work. Since the late 1980s, when offshore production became the norm, most designers and retailers don't own the factories that manufacture their stock, and instead subcontract across the supply chain. Retailers hire manufacturers, who hire contractors, who hire subcontractors, who hire garment workers. Retailers claim no responsibility for workers, and only the profitable factories are continually sought out. The farther a company or consumer distances itself from a problem, the less responsible one feels. Because clothing companies don't own factories, and are often not privy to poor working conditions, they are also legally distanced from suppliers.

Just as synthetics have enabled fast fashion companies to produce massive volumes of clothing, globalization and rapidly increasing production have facilitated a downward spiral in wages. Most brands won't pay more than a country's minimum wage, plus any mandated overtime. This leaves workers around the world competing against each other. In many places, like Pakistan and Bangladesh, and even in Los Angeles, many garment workers do not make a living wage, let alone a minimum wage.

Manufacturing clothes even at an industrial scale is a labour intensive process. Labour is a large proportion of production costs, at around 20-40%. Because of the labour intensive nature of making clothes, the price we pay to sewing machine operators and other factory workers greatly affects retail prices. Making fast fashion clothing requires cheap labour, with wages driven as low as possible. In an industry which makes enormous profits, it would seem feasible to pay a reasonable and fair wage.

The domestic manufacturing base in North America and other countries can't compete with the low wages of developing countries. Even the workers who make our clothes in North and South America suffer from low wages. In Marketplace's episode *"Hidden Price of Your Clothes"* it was found that in the Fashion District of Los Angeles, 45,000 workers were not paid minimum wage, and most were immigrant workers.

Along with the global problem of being chronically underpaid, workers may have to face working long hours, and in extreme cases 80 hours per week. They also face occupational and health hazards, and forced labour has been documented in China; more recently the struggles of the Uyghurs working in cotton production. Sweatshop environments still exist today, even in Britain and the US, and are typically staffed by immigrants.

Toxic effluents and air pollutants associated with textile manufacturing processes, especially dyeing and finishing, are dangerous sectors to work in. Not only has textile waste caused an environmental catastrophe, but it also affects the health of workers, particularly in those areas that accept clothing surplus. Two of the largest hubs for used and unsold garments are Ghana and Chile. What doesn't get used or sold in markets often gets incinerated, releasing toxic substances into the air. The Kantamanto Market in Accra, Ghana accepts 15 million garments every week, contributing to the local textile industry. But around 40% of the items are of such poor quality that they are either landfilled or burned.

Today, consumers are also at risk for health problems associated with residual toxic chemicals used in the manufacture of clothing. A class of chemicals known as *"forever chemicals"* are finding their way into clothing. PFAS (polyfluoroalkyl substances), a group of compounds containing fluorine are prevalent in some brands of outdoor apparel, athletic wear like leggings and sports bras, and fire-fighting gear. These compounds hang around for a long time. Some manufacturers apply PFAS-based finishes to the outer layer of clothes and uniforms to make them water and stain resistant. CBC reported recently that Health Canada and Environment Canada propose listing human-made chemicals as toxic under the Canadian Environmental Protection Act (CEPA), including PFAS.

Most of the well-known luxury brands like Louis Vuitton and Chanel began as exclusive, creating custom goods for individuals with the help of a team of skilled workers. Sewing and other textile crafts, such as beadwork and embroidery, were respected professions that required years of training. In these environments, collaboration with the designer was part of the job, and workers felt involved in the process of creating garments. That's not to say that workers in mass production factories had no struggles, but the garment workers often had unions that could fight for their rights and negotiate for better wages. Today, the artisans of couture work is becoming a dying art, and many young people aren't interested in these jobs. Even designers are hired hands.

Sewing jobs today are equated to sweatshops and human suffering. Sewing is now considered to be lousy work, with most of the labour done in modular style production facilities. Clothing is handmade goods broken down into assembly line steps. Each worker focuses on one element of the garment-making process, and your job is one or a few tasks performed all-day, such as setting in sleeves, attaching zippers, steam finishing, or inspecting pieces for final quality. The work is tedious and there is no collaboration with designers. This division of labour creates a disconnect from the art of making clothes. The task-based work doesn't require as much training, and each step is usually performed by young women. Sewing should be a great job, but for many garment workers around the globe, it is a struggle just to survive.

In countries like Africa, the clothing and textile by-products imported from around the world wreak havoc on the local economies, and are partly responsible for the demise of local arts and crafts. The artisans can't compete with the low prices, and for some, Western clothing is often seen as more fashionable than the local items.

The point of this chapter was not to delve into the specifics of the damaging effects of fashion production, but to discuss them in a broader context. The alarming rate and excessive amount of fashion clothing produced is one of the most serious problems we are faced with. Overproduction happens regardless of our consumptive habits, and one third of what's produced, never gets sold. Fashion's predominant business model is destroying the environment, humanity's future, and diminishing the value of clothing. Fashion's supply chain is designed to create newness, but is at odds with doing the right thing for the environment and people. It's time to change. But how do we make change?

Chapter 5

Minimizing Fashion's Footprint

"Waste is a design flaw." author unknown

What is sustainability?

The United Nations states that *"Sustainability is the means to maintain change in a balanced environment without compromising future needs. It's a combination of social, economic, and environmental needs"*. Sustainability encompasses the environment, economic and social discussions because they are inextricably linked. As humans we are intimately tied to nature, and because of this our positive or negative actions influence our eco-system. Sustainability is not a new concept and people have always applied sustainable principles to their life and work.

"Sustainable fashion" refers to clothing and accessories that are manufactured and accessed in an ecologically and socially responsible manner. *"Eco-friendly"* or *"green"* fashion is a clear focus on leaving minimal damage to the environment. *"Ethical fashion"* is more focused on the people working in the fashion supply chain, including actions that are taken to combat racism, low wages, exploitive conditions, farmers' well-being, and the ill effects of toxic manufacturing processes.

To be *"sustainable"* requires a holistic approach. This entails rethinking the way clothing is manufactured including, producing fabrics with conscious materials, incorporating cellulose-based fibres from regenerative practices, and the use of natural and less toxic dyes and finishes. Responsible use of resources and ethical labour standards is part of the mix. Sustainability in all its entirety can feel overwhelming, and is a tall order.

On an optimistic note, there is an awakening interest in sustainability among consumers of fashion, and those working in the industry. The fashion industry knows it's having an impact on the environment and humans, as evident by global sustainability fashion events, advocacy groups, and organizations. The irony is that large conglomerates keep manufacturing at an alarming rate, which is limiting the industry's ability to develop better practices. Adding to the problem of excess production, just about every process in textile manufacturing has side effects. Fashion can never be 100% green, but globally, there is consensus as to what "*sustainability*" is and what impacts need to be measured. The fashion industry has been slow to respond, and thanks to organizations like the UK's Fashion Revolution, and select designers and manufacturers, the conversation has begun.

What's holding the fashion industry back?
Fragmented Supply Chain

Fashion is unique in that it intersects with many other industries, including the agriculture behind leather, cotton, cellulose-based fibres, wool, and other sources of raw materials, as well as fossil fuels, chemicals required for dyeing and finishing, transportation of goods, retailers, and textile recycling. But at the same time, the business of fashion is disconnected from all of these sectors.

Fashion is also integrated into the global economy. Most companies do not own their manufacturing facilities, resulting in a gap between brands and suppliers, with middlemen engaging in subcontracting. This approach devalues the process of making clothes, and the people who make our clothes. Companies have little control over the sourcing of raw materials, the manufacturing processes, or the industry's workers. Not only is the supply chain huge and fragmented, but many brands are controlled by fashion conglomerates. It becomes particularly challenging for these large fashion companies to pivot and engage in sustainable practices, without realizing the immense profits they're used to.

My research data from the late 1990s showed that most small Canadian companies found its size to be an advantage, allowing them to have control and flexibility in adapting to a changing environment. This holds true today, as more smaller companies are applying sustainable goals and practices. There are only a handful of large fashion companies that are making the changes necessary for a healthier planet.

Flawed Business Model

The predominant business model in fashion is a linear one, *"take-make-dispose"*, a system where sustainable fashion can't exist. Fashion's business model is depleting natural resources at an alarming rate to overproduce clothing that ultimately ends up in the landfill. Fashion prioritizes profit; exploitive of labour and people. In the book *"The Day The World Stops Shopping"*, MacKinnon says *"the greatest danger for the garment trade is not a slowdown in shopping, but a failure to find a way to slow down shopping"*.

Fast fashion generates unnecessary demand for clothing, by accelerating fashion trends, and making clothes cheap enough for consumers to buy more and more. The low prices attached to fast fashion, only makes people gravitate to it. In a hyper-manufacturing world corners are cut, diminishing the quality of garments, and companies easily engage in exploitive and damaging practices. And little thought is given to the externalities produced by the fashion industry.

The production of clothing has doubled over the past 20 years, and if companies continue with this strategy of exponential growth of more products, more sales, and easier buying, any sustainable efforts made negates progress. It doesn't matter how good the materials may be, if a company continues to fill the market with too much clothing, nothing changes. Companies used to emphasize the design and manufacturing processes, but now it's more about marketing products and brand identity, focusing on the values that sell a product versus the product itself. The fashion business is no longer about "*making*" clothes, but more about "*selling*" them.

Largely an Unregulated Industry

Totally free, opaque markets leads to a slew of problems, and within an unregulated industry there are no obligations or incentives for the fashion industry to change their damaging business practices. Having a more structured environment in which to work in, allows companies to know the basics from which to operate, and prevents a mishmash of solutions. It is difficult to regulate such a huge and globalized supply chain, but legislation is absolutely necessary to motivate change.

Outside accreditation from independent companies does exist in this industry, primarily in the category of sustainable materials, or fibres and fabrications made in a responsible way. The following are some of the available certifications:

Oeko-Tex - provides independent certificates and product labels representing products which are safe, environmentally friendly, and manufactured in a socially responsible way.

Fair Trade Textile Standard - promotes sustainable development, and reduces poverty through fairer trade, by guaranteeing a decent living, ensuring employers are paid a living wage, allowing the formation of unions, and adhering to health and safety principles.

Cradle-to-Cradle Certified® - a global standard for products that are safe, circular, and responsibly made, across five categories of sustainable performance: material health, product circularity (regenerative products and process design), clean air and climate protection, promoting renewable energy and reducing emissions, water and soil stewardship, and social fairness.

Bluesign® - main goal is to motivate suppliers, manufacturers, and brands to reduce the overall footprint of textiles, with a focus on the chemicals used. They offer service packages for manufacturers, brands and retailers to help identify goals and monitor progress.

These certifications are voluntary and come at a high cost, with plenty of paperwork required to accurately label products. Every step of the supply chain needs to be checked. It's a self-regulatory burden for companies with too many ways to mess up, and not something that most companies are willing to navigate, particularly fast fashion companies.

Bad Data and Misinformation

Fashion is a product that is often misunderstood as a driver of climate change. Clothing is often missed when having the conversation about lessening our footprint. People have embraced changing food habits, and reducing single-use plastic waste in their homes and businesses, but we don't know or don't care about the plastic in our clothing, or the mounting textile waste in landfills.

Fashion is not exempt from our crazy world filled with misinformation. A very small percentage of cited facts about fashion's footprint is based on science, data collection, or peer-reviewed research. Most of the information accessed is based on gut feelings, broken links, marketing messages, false facts spreading through social media, or something someone said years ago. Academics shy away from doing scientific research in this industry. Any research is often published and funded by brands, leaving flawed references or what methodologies were used in acquiring data. When you work in or study fashion, you are often asked *"when will you be getting a real job?"*. Yet clothing plays such a significant role in our identity, and reveals much about the culture in which we live.

The industry needs research and solid data about water pollution, carbon emissions, waste pollution, and the human costs. Without good data about fashion's true impact, misinformation and disinformation prevents progress in mitigating climate change and implementing regulations. A lack of data stymies collective action, and if nobody knows how bad things are, it is hard to demand better.

No Definition of Sustainability

The word *"sustainable"* along with other buzzwords like *"ethical"*, *"green"*, *"eco-friendly"* and *"responsibly made"* suffers from ambiguity. All of these words lack concrete definitions with foundations in law that customers and brands can observe. Because these words are overused, they lose value and meaning.

Today, sustainable fashion encompasses many things including: climate impacts, labour and human issues, chemical use, microplastic pollution, waste, and regenerative farming. For many large brands, there is a tendency to focus on one element of sustainability, like using organic cotton, or a small percentage of recycled fibre, conflating environmental damage with sustainability. Because we have already degraded our systems, some experts say that focusing on sustainability is not the right mindset. If we sustain the systems where they are, they will never be resilient.

Actions Don't Jive With Beliefs

As humans we tend to go beyond our immediate needs; a surplus of food, shelter, clothing, and other commodities. We have never seen such an exorbitant amount of clothing produced and sold for so little. Seeing poor quality clothes sell for such low prices, shows how little we value what we wear, and the people who make our clothes. These lower prices encourage shoppers to cycle through clothes more quickly.

Brands that make one small change, but continue to produce and commit damaging practices, are not embracing the shift that's required to deal with fashion's problems, regardless of any initiative made. This only causes confusion and convinces consumers that the problem is getting better.

Contrary to consumers demanding more sustainable products, we still purchase too much. Prime example is the world's most profitable online clothing company, Shein, the latest entry into fast fashion, coined *"ultra-fast fashion"*. It's everything bad about fast fashion, pushing high volume, relentless pace and low prices to the absolute extreme. With the help of technology, Shein's clothing collections are released daily, and market fashion hauls are displayed on TikTok. Generation Z claim they are concerned about the environment, but is the target customer for ultra-cheap fashion. It's very difficult to alter behaviour, when our perceptions of products are primarily used to look good for one specific event or a photo-op, and nothing short of wasteful.

The Myth of Recycling

Two of the most difficult technologies to address is textile recycling, and designing closed-loop systems. Recycling is a short term solution. The truth is recycling can't be looked at as an easy answer to fashion's sustainability problems. Everyday, we take clothing to donation centres or drop it in the trash, believing that somewhere along the chain it will be *"recycled"*.

The word *"recycling"* is problematic, when what we're doing in our homes is sorting clothing, typically collected for resale and not recycling. Recycling is a term that carries wide meaning for people, but is often used to describe the many ways of dealing with waste. Today, the journey of a piece of clothing does not always end up in landfill. Recycling often happens in three ways: clothing is resold to consumers at lower prices, exported in bulk to developing countries for sale, and chemically or mechanically recycled into raw materials.

True recycling means converting materials into something approximating the same value as the original, by reducing or breaking down a product into its component materials, and making something new. Recycling puts the materials back into a similar product. A good example, is recycling scraps of fabric into its component threads to create new cloth.

Currently, less than 1% of clothing is actually recycled into new fibres. The majority of our fabrics are blended or composed of more than one fibre. This new area of technology has yet to figure out how to separate different fibres, and recycle them into high quality ones. To date most recyclers of textile products are only able to use fabrics with 100% fibre content or mono-fibre fabrics, leaving a lot of textile waste that can't be broken down. Another challenge to recycling is preventing each new fibre cycle from becoming shorter and weaker. There is also the additional problem of all the other components added to clothing that need to be removed before recycling.

Much of the recycling to date is really downcycling. 12% of textile waste is downcycled into less valuable items, such as insulation materials, mattress filling or cloth rags. Sometimes downcycling increases contaminants in the environment, because other chemicals are often added to make the materials useful again. Downcycling can even be more expensive for businesses, because it forces some materials into more lifetimes, using more energy and other resources than what they were originally designed for.

95% of the recycled polyester used in fabric production comes from PET bottles, rather than from recycling polyester clothing and textiles. Using plastic bottles should really be used for making new bottles rather than clothing, to truly close the loop and be sustainable. Recycling is an energy intensive industrial process and expensive. Some brands have introduced fully recyclable garments, but comes with high costs, and has yet to reach scale. With the sheer volume of clothing, a lack of infrastructure, the huge investment requirement, and the legislation needed to scale up fashion, recycling is not the best solution, and should be considered the last option. Consumer awareness of the fate of clothing through its lifecycle, may be the best hope for a more sustainable fashion industry.

The Effects of These Problems

Fashion's intersection with so many industries, of which they have little control, leads to lack of transparency over even the most basic information, making it difficult to determine fashion's true footprint. With no recognized definition of sustainability, or agreed upon means of measuring what a sustainable brand is, the term is left to interpretation by individuals and companies, resulting in different solutions, goals, and objectives. A new trend noted by the organization, Fashion Revolution, is *"green-hushing"*; companies choosing not to be transparent about their climate goals to avoid allegations of greenwashing.

Greenwashing refers to brands which make incomplete, inaccurate or misleading claims, implying that they are making products and engaging in practices, which appear more responsible than they actually are. Greenwashing is common within large fast fashion brands, which use these claims to balance out their negative impact. When H&M calls a product *"conscious"* because it contains 75% recycled polyester, 16% acrylic, and 9% wool, they are eliminating important information - that 9% wool content is not adding any benefit. And when they give you a coupon to purchase new clothes in exchange for dropping off old ones in a donation bin, they are enticing you to buy more.

The ambiguity surrounding the word *"sustainable"* and the other problems outlined in the previous section, leads to a significant amount of greenwashing, such as distorting the truth about the materials which comprise clothing. The use of recycled synthetics like rPET is often blended with virgin plastic, and promoted to the public as a viable circular option. This option doesn't guarantee that the garment is biodegradable, circular or recyclable, and delays progress on reducing plastic.

There are many steps to clothing production, and brands often consider only one design feature or characteristic, leaving out other essential information, and calling the collection conscious or sustainable. Meanwhile, companies continue to focus on overproduction, exploitation of workers, and polluting the environment. It's easy to say something is sustainable and not have to prove it. Greenwashing creates a lot of noise, confusion and distrust.

Fast fashion and social media are huge marketing machines, and they use ambiguity to sell the feeling of responsibility. Greenwashing is all about marketing products as more green than they really are, and messaging plays a huge role in our consumption patterns. It's not just the communication from brands, but also from style segments on popular television talk shows, and social media influencers, who all like to focus on low price points, making us believe we are one shop away from fashion nirvana.

Building a Better Fashion System
The inherent nature of change in fashion is at odds with sustainability. The mass production of clothing is not new, but has accelerated over the decades. What is relatively new is the concept of disposability. We see our thrown out items disappear when the garbage truck picks them up, or those exported to the global secondhand trade. In times past, a culture's mindset kept clothing as long as possible, repairing, altering, or handing down. In its present form, the fashion industry is an unjust and unsustainable one.

To minimize fashion's footprint demands nothing less than a transformation. If you like, a *"rethink"* of almost everything, including different business models, challenging the concept of sustainability, and taking a more holistic approach. Inclusive of this approach is questioning growth, slowing down production, developing policies and legislation, changing our habits and finding new ways of making meaning in our lives, fostering collaboration within and outside of the industry for new ideas and possible solutions.

Economics of Degrowth

The elephant in the room that fashion businesses like to avoid, is the concept of degrowth. In capitalistic markets the objective is to endlessly expand the consumer economy. The answer to why your company exists is not growth, but is only a result. If you're building a company based solely on growth, things like ethics and quality will surely suffer, and a mindset such as this does not build a successful business. The key will be to challenge the idea of growth as a main indicator of success, and redefine the meaning of prosperity. Companies must reduce the volume of products created to alleviate excess, and decrease consumption.

In the existing linear structure, companies can't possibly do the right thing for the environment. You can have a viable business with less speed or what some are already achieving - versions of *"slow fashion"*. Most of the conscious fashion created now is made up of independent, small companies, and by only a handful of large companies like Patagonia and Eileen Fisher.

Focusing on growth as the main indicator of economic success has led to its rewards enjoyed unevenly in the population with a lot of inequity. This type of strategy doesn't take into account the social and economic costs to the economy. A healthy economy is impossible without the health and well-being of people, and a positive relationship with the environment. Achieving a better definition of what growth means for your company is the first step. Change is possible by carrying out different strategies like the ones suggested below, and adjusting a fashion company's infrastructure.

Better Design and Manufacturing of Clothing

Fast fashion has become normalized, and our behaviour is limited by the choices we are given. Modifying the negligent practices of fashion's supply chain begins with designing and constructing durable, beautiful goods that are made to last much longer than they presently do.

Sustainable, good fashion design should be about maintaining a balance between a designer's expression, while respecting consumer needs, industry workers, and all the other elements involved in the design and manufacturing of clothing. At present, there is little circular design in the fashion industry, other than different variations of recycling. Circular economies focus on reusing, repurposing, and recycling materials to reduce consumption of natural resources, and avoid creation of waste. The ideal future of circularity is fibre-to-fibre recycled garments - taking a cotton shirt which can be turned into yarn to make a new garment.

An organic design process is slow and intentional. The goal of manufacturers is to design better products at all price points, including the concepts of durability and longevity, and perhaps a return to seasonal collections. Clothes need to be kept in circulation longer, with waste incorporated into the lifecycle of the product. There will always be waste in fashion, but that doesn't mean an afterlife strategy can't be found. Smart choices made early on in the design process leads to better recycling in the future. Increasing the number of times clothing is worn is an effective solution, and moving clothes out of the closet to a more responsible place.

Brands need to source materials that do the least damage. This is challenging because there are so many variables and priorities for companies. There is no best material, so it's critical to find what characteristics are important to you as a designer or manufacturer, and work these into the design process. Leadership can provide specific goals and sustainable parameters that are appropriate for either small or large companies, as well as for the types of products they make.

In choosing natural or synthetic fibres, every choice comes with trade-offs. That being said, the global fibre market places too much emphasis on fossil fuel synthetics. I would love to see a resurgent growth in natural fibres, like wool, linen, hemp, organic cotton that use regenerative farming practices, and an overall increase in mono-fibre fabrications. Choosing natural fibres ensures biodegradability, and regenerative agriculture benefits local ecosystems and economies, as well as preserving traditional crafts.

The only advantage polyester or other synthetics have had in the manufacture of clothing is cost. It is recommended to reduce the use of synthetics unless they are recycled, dead stock (leftover fabrics from production), or is absolutely essential to the performance of the item. A renewed interest in natural fibres addresses the overuse of one fibre over another, but also the social and environmental challenges. Scaling up technology of bio-synthetics and plant-based materials decreases the cost of entry, but is also a better alternative to synthetics. The industry needs more development in technology for chemical recycling of fabrics and yarns into high quality fibres for new clothing. This would be the best solution for fast fashion brands, which could take back their clothes, and use them as raw materials to make new collections. Reselling strategies only work for brands that make high quality clothing. Developing relationships with textile mills, consumers, and others along the supply chain increases transparency. Fostering collaboration by joining forces within and outside of the industry can only improve practices and promote business.

Managing Waste

Clothing is utilitarian, and eventually wears out. As with all consumer products, waste is inevitable. Style obsolescence is a driver of fashion, and the instigator of waste. At present, there are no reasonable solutions for end-of-life, other than keeping clothing in circulation longer, and reducing the amount of clothing made. Choosing the easiest sustainable solutions like using mono-fibre fabrics doesn't change end of life. Although fabrics made of natural fibres biodegrade, and is a more responsible choice, there are the other components used in sewing clothes like trims, buttons, and zippers which affect end-of-life. These are nuances that manufacturers need to consider when making decisions based on their objectives.

In dealing with waste, it's urgent to reduce the amount produced and consumed, and to extend the longevity of goods. Designing with better materials increases viability for more than a season, and promotes the implementation of closed loop systems in the supply chain.

The next frontier in waste management is textiles. There are only a few urban centres in Canada that have implemented city-wide textile waste programs known as *"textile recycling"* that divert clothes from the landfill. At present, textile waste programs consist of donating clothing to charities and thrift stores, which sort and grade clothes, and sell wholesale to the public, and to secondhand markets overseas. Some do mechanical recycling. Textile recycling is not at scale, and downcycling is more common. Some textile waste companies are imaginative, selling kits filled with remnants for use in a variety of DIY projects, or by offering repair classes. Not many programs pass on well-used clothes to recyclers, most of which end up in global secondhand markets.

Some retailers provide in-store garment collection bins for cast-offs, and a handful of retailers have take-back programs for repairs and reselling. The most well-known is Worn Wear offered by Patagonia. Eileen Fisher also operates the Renew program, which takes back their garments to be reused, recycled or remade into collections that are resold in dedicated Renew stores.

Policies and Legislation

Actions should be tied into what we need to do about climate change, and no one action is a cure-all. Legislating the fashion industry requires involvement by all participants in fashion: citizens, political leaders, policy makers, brands, journalists, and other media to address and manage transparency, greenwashing, and misinformation. Transparency itself is not sustainability, but provides incentive to make change. Establishing policies, necessitates collaboration between a wide spectrum of voices. Legislation provides infrastructure, with guidelines and regulations to assist companies in establishing goals and objectives, towards better decision making around sustainable practices. Rules are set for what businesses can and can't do, workplace protections, and funding for research and development. Policies and legislation will alleviate companies deciding for themselves what sustainability is. And it also means companies are held accountable for environmental impacts with enforcement that penalizes inaction.

France has a long history of supporting fashion and leads the way in legislating the industry. There is ongoing discussion of laws, which require companies to reuse or recycle their products. The French government passed a law in 2020, prohibiting the destruction and unnecessary waste of unsold merchandise. The EU is also engaging in discussions of reducing waste and cracking down on greenwashing. Great Britain has long held conservation and environmental initiatives, and most recently the *"Why Wool Matters"* campaign, revitalizing the use of wool in textiles to reduce the demand for synthetics. The UK's Green Claims Code holds that brands must substantiate any claims of product sustainability, and if found guilty of greenwashing, they could be in breach of consumer protection laws. California's Garment Worker Protection Act took effect in January, 2022, intended to result in fair wages, and improved working conditions. New York City is working on the Fashion Sustainability and Social Accountability Act, and when passed aims to hold major brands accountable for environmental and social impacts. A new bill initiated by World Vision of Canada aims to curb child and forced labour in the supply chain, requiring companies to report the use of forced or child labour.

Change is easier with a structure in place. Investing in increased transparency across the supply chain, increases the accessibility of factual information for the public, and businesses to make better choices. In addition to increased transparency, a by-product of legislation entices more scientists, climate experts, and other professionals to show an interest in fashion, which would greatly benefit the industry.

Living Wages

The reality is that wages are so low, and companies profits are so high, that wages could be raised without passing the cost on to the consumers. Clothing companies have enjoyed decades of cheap labour and profits, with questionable benefits to consumers. Domestic manufacturing bases can't compete with wages in the global south. Raising wages in these countries would allow us to compete on a fairer playing field. It's a vicious cycle of cheap labour, more garments, more shopping, and more profit. It's been shown that adding a few cents per garment sewn can make a difference for workers.

Regulatory frameworks must include living wages for those who make our clothes, those involved in the production of fibres, and an investment in regenerative farming. Fashion's business viability, and what's best for the industry overrides what's best for the most vulnerable. Brands and retailers typically don't consider the needs of workers, and those most vulnerable aren't able to live the lifestyle they want, yet the west carries on with their exploitive ways.

Policy makers need to better evaluate the socio-economic impact of fibre production. Farmers should be able to continue with what works for them to increase yield, and not be forced to try different crops, that companies think are beneficial.

Throughout history, environmental groups like PETA and

other fashion interest groups, have at times negatively interfered with local economies. *The New Report: The Great Greenwashing Machine (2021)* found that alpaca sales are the sole cash crop of the poorest residents in Peru, but in 2020 PETA released a video of some rogue shearer at a Peruvian alpaca farm, that raised eyebrows. Nothing but a distraction, this act affected livelihoods, by decreasing the sales of alpaca fibre. History shows similar scenarios played out in Canada, where environmentalists who misunderstood the relationship between Inuit and nature, decimated the fur trapping trade.

Traditional crafts and skills, predominant in many areas around the world are under-appreciated, and many artisans don't benefit from their talent and skills. These communities should be protected within legal frameworks. Mass produced fashion hurts the livelihood of artisans and craftspeople, because of the shift to mechanized factories, and low paid labour. Industrialization created sweatshops and global inequities.

The future of employees is certainly a question to ask when moving towards creating a more circular future for fashion. Because there will be job losses, people will need alternative livelihoods, by diversifying and integrating their skills into a new system. This could be a great opportunity to have healthier work environments with more purpose, better lifestyles, and an increase in local economies.

Shifting Mindset and Behaviour

A cultural shift is the antidote to heal our broken relationship with clothing. Changing the way we think about our clothes is central to this shift. People need to feel part of the solution, rather than making them feel guilty for what they are not doing. Clothing plays a huge role in our identity, and our place in the world. Shopping less is a harm reduction strategy, but also motivates shoppers to think twice about their habits, and makes us more accountable. Addressing a shift in behaviour, brand messaging, transparency, and being able to trace the history of what we buy, will move us in the right direction.

Brand advertising should inspire positive action, such as how to care for and repair products. Too much focus is placed on value, convenience, and the need for more and more clothes to live better, and that clothes need to be replaced, rather than promoting quality over quantity, and a unique sense of style.

We need to know that brands are accountable for all those who contribute to production through transparency. Garment labels don't tell the whole story. 96% of manufacturers do not indicate whose making their products, or if workers are receiving a living wage. Educate consumers through business platforms, that describe where the raw materials originate from, where the clothes are made and by whom, and the workplace conditions.

We used to understand the geography known for certain design and manufacturing skills. Italy produced the finest woollens and leather goods. Germans were skilled in design and tailored construction. The best linen was grown in France. Scotland was infamous for cashmere goods and woven paisley. China and India produced the best silk textiles. Because the supply chain is transnational, we don't understand the characteristics of clothes that depend on the materials and the places they are sewn. And the most exclusive clothing and accessories are far removed from us.

It is even more challenging to be transparent because of the many different steps that take place across the supply chain. Conveying traceable information on labels should be easily understood, like the information provided on food labels, and other consumer products. For the consumer, it's about a balance between a love for fashion, and an interest in saving the planet, through conscious consumption. A conscious effort means shifting our habits, finding new ways of making meaning in our lives, holding brands and policy makers accountable, supporting a movement for change, and applying pressure by asking good questions.

Education

To deal with misinformation and inaccurate data, research by academics and the industry is critical in helping companies define their goals and objectives towards sustainability. More accurate estimates of environmental impacts and quality data allows companies to track and measure outputs that can be passed on to consumers. Studying other fields for ideas, possible solutions, and past sustainable efforts provide new perspectives, ideas, and solutions.

In fashion schools, the main focus of study is more often on the designer and manufacturer, or the celebrity around designer collections. To change the way fashion is made, a fashion curriculum should increase students awareness of all the fields of expertise required to make fashion; textile scientists for innovative fabrications, farmers and fibre production, skills of traditional craftspeople, designing with minimal waste, and using recycled materials. Brands can educate consumers on various topics related to their products, that isn't greenwashing.

I had home economics in junior high school, which taught me valuable skills, like garment construction and mending. But educating young kids today can go beyond mending; introduce them to the industry, the science behind textiles, and what sustainability should look like.

Alternative Business Models

There are many start-ups and existing companies around the world that have shifted their business models, and developed strategies towards more social responsibility and minimizing fashion's damages to the environment. Along with the solutions to the structural problems outlined in the last section, including legislation and defining sustainable parameters, it is daunting for companies to figure out where to start with so much to consider. It takes time to transition, so begin with something challenging but achievable. Outline your sustainable priorities, but only deal with a few changes at a time, so that your focus is narrow and achievable, before moving on to the next stage. You might choose to deal with textile waste, or use only natural fibres in your products. Paying living wages should be a standard, and never compromised. In the end, sustainable fashion should be thought of in terms of longevity, not cost.

The following are alternative business models; some are ideas and solutions that existed in previous decades, tweaked to adjust to the modern world. The best hope for a better fashion industry is to move from a linear model to a more circular one, which entails returning our cast-offs back into the system. This quote from Peter Seegar says it all; *"If it can't be reduced, reused, repaired, refurbished, resold, recycled or composted; **then it should be** restricted, redesigned, removed from production."*

No business model can be 100% sustainable, but these models offer financial stability and better ways of meeting the needs of communities, and are more in tune with what customers want.

Cooperative Organizational Structure

As a teenager, I worked in a co-op retailer, and it felt good to receive a monetary bonus, because I had a share of ownership in the company. All who work in a cooperative have a stake in decision-making and ownership. In fashion cooperatives, all makers profit from the manufacture of products.

Social Enterprise

The core focus of this business model is for a positive social impact. These types of enterprises, promote unique skills, and are often led by artisans in traditional communities. There are two brands of knitting yarns I love which are hand-dyed in the local tradition of the South American countries, Uruguay and Peru. Some hand-knitting companies collaborate with these artisan communities, to make products for their clients world wide. These types of enterprises keep craft traditions alive in these areas, appreciating the cultural value and beauty of each specific art form. These businesses are a refreshing alternative to the factory conditions, that predominate the fashion industry.

Designing and Manufacturing With Existing Waste - Upcycling

This type of fashion design company utilizes "*waste*" from all types of textile sources including fabric, yarn, and existing garments, to form new fashion products, and upcycled items. Some examples include felting old wool sweaters, then cutting and stitching the felt to make new items, or using fabric scraps to make patchwork and appliqué bags. This is a great solution for incorporating waste into the lifecycle of a product, which is key to a more circular economy.

The Sharing Economy

This model takes advantage of clothing already in the marketplace. There is a resurgence of vintage sellers, secondhand clothing stores, online resale outlets, rental shops, borrowing and swapping events. The positive feature of this business model is that clothing is kept in circulation longer. Some large companies have incorporated secondhand portals into their business; the two most well-known programs are offered by Patagonia and Eileen Fisher. They hire a company that inspects, cleans, and repairs their branded items people send back, and the refurbished ones go back on sale through the brand's stores and online sites.

Recently H&M and Zara added secondhand portals. The problem is that fast fashion resale programs don't change fast fashion's environmental footprint, because they still overproduce. It's simply another cash cow; no real change is made by creating another avenue for selling goods, which only increases consumption. Resale models require items of quality and longevity. If brands want to enter the resale market; the clothes must stand up or this strategy won't work. Fast fashion companies layering resale into their product offerings, must be paired with a commitment to change, otherwise it's simply lip service.

Service Based Businesses

Another model intent on keeping clothes and accessories in circulation are companies offering repairs and tailoring services. In past decades, tailors and seamstresses offered custom-made clothing, but today these professionals are more associated with altering services. These service businesses also include personalized style companies, for organizing and caring for what you already own. These are great services that have been declining over the years, but hopefully a comeback is in store.

Custom Fashion

Custom and *"couture"* fashion is a type of slow fashion that makes clothing to each client's specifications. There is no excess created by overproduction, resulting in an overall reduction in waste. With an increase in the use of quality materials, skilled labour, and service, more time and effort is put in by the designer, and sewers are appreciated. It's a move away from instant gratification, and the customer appreciates having something unique to them. Jean-Paul Gaultier, a well-known haute couture designer, has shifted his business model to one of couture, bowing out of the frenetic ready-to-wear industry. Not only do haute couture designers create custom pieces, but smaller, local designers are choosing this niche business model.

Designing Fewer Collections

Another model that's slow and intentional are companies creating one or two collections per year, prioritizing quality over quantity. Over the last few years, I've patronized a local, small design company that produces a couple of collections per year. I love the quality of the fabrics, the fit, longevity, and the originality of the pieces. And by having fewer choices, it is easier to purchase what works for me.

Even though these types of businesses resist fast fashion's growth and profit narrative, what is noticeable with these alternatives, is that they are inherently more localized, manufacture on a smaller scale, and maintain financial stability. Big is not always better, and many a small company regret having merged. Scale is what caused so many of fashion's problems. Sustainable, local manufacturing is not scaleable but is easily replicated, allowing for innovation, increased competition, and greater control over the business. Small manufacturing companies also tend to hire local workers.

In order to improve the fashion system, the focus turns to the customer; companies benefit not only by selling clothes, but by selling perks along the way. Relationships develop with customers, leading to customer loyalty and added value. Customer loyalty is a characteristic that is crucial to all businesses, but is more apparent with these alternative ones.

For all businesses that are working on or becoming more sustainable, take customers along on your journey. Communicating the numbers and metrics to prove what you are doing, and revealing the general strategy of your brand, customers can then make informed purchases. Brands can further educate clients, not only by showing sustainable efforts, but by giving advice on topics, like caring for their product offerings.

Even though my theses is dated, what still applies is that joint efforts made within flexible business networks enhances opportunities, and increased competitiveness with larger companies. Networking within the fashion industry and with local businesses benefits local economies. At the time I had a retail store, the surrounding businesses easily engaged in cooperative marketing programs, without the fear of competition.

A question that comes to mind is *"Can large fast fashion*

brands ever be sustainable?" My answer to this is "*no*", with a caveat. No, because fast fashion has taken its problems to new levels: widespread labour exploitation, ecological degradation, and an exponential increase in textile waste. Large fast fashion brands tend to focus on sustainable materials, and even then are limited to a small number of items in collections, with negligible amounts of quality materials. But they continually overproduce with weekly or daily collections, and chase the cheapest production costs. If these companies slowed down production, they wouldn't be fast fashion anymore - a conundrum indeed.

Big fashion brands won't save us, but improvement is warranted. They have the wealth to do better in many areas such as funding research, and developing technology for the production of biomaterials, new fabrications, and scaling textile recycling. A greater level of control over the processes along the supply chain, will incentivize them towards greener solutions, as well as a greater level of transparency. Doing so, would potentially make conscious fashion more widespread, and bring down prices to truly democratize fashion.

Now it's time to put together the science behind our fabrics, and the best sustainable practices, to structure a more conscious wardrobe. One that you can be proud of, and know you are doing good for the planet. Let's begin your journey with the characteristics of well-made clothing.

Chapter 6

What makes for a quality piece of clothing?

"Only an excellent fabric can originate an excellent fashion." Nino Cerruti

Quality is perceived by each of us differently. I have an affinity to natural fibres, especially wool and silk, textured woven fabric, hand-knits, and unique construction details. Price does not guide my decision making, but I won't pay a high designer price for a basic item like a T-shirt, or for an acrylic sweater that pills excessively and stretches out of shape. I avoid fast fashion retailers, and try not to make impulsive purchases. Our clothing choices vary with context, circumstance, age, income, mood, and what *"value"* means to us. But now for many of us clothing's value is based on price alone.

At times, you may have thought that *"things aren't made the same anymore"*. When it comes to consumer products including clothing, there is truth to this statement. Quality clothing has declined, partly because we have so many choices with vast differences in levels of quality. In the past we had fewer options for replacements, and people from all income levels took a certain pride in caring for their clothes, altering and repairing them to keep them longer, and wore them till they fell apart. Today we've learned to expect clothing to be inexpensive, and as a consequence, formed an addiction to purchasing more items for less, as Winner's advertising tagline so aptly describes our consumptive habit *"Find Fabulous For Less."*

It's not an easy task to search for quality items in a sea of choices, and learning to spot quality won't happen overnight. A good place to begin is by exposing yourself to well-made clothes and those not so well-made, comparing fabrics with differing levels of quality, and the variety of construction methods. Walk into diverse retailers, including vintage stores and examine the different offerings. Try items on to check fit and construction. Look at your own clothes and establish what quality means to you, determine how long your clothes typically last, and study how garments are sewn together.

I'm lucky to have grown up in a time when it was easier to find quality clothing at affordable prices. My mother's best friend was a skilled seamstress, a German woman who was taught by the best in her home country. She could whip up leather shorts for her boys, and sew together an Astrakhan 3/4 coat without a purchased pattern. She made much of my mother's wardrobe, and taught me the characteristics of well-made clothes. The most important lesson we can learn from wearing quality garments is their classic appeal and longevity. Classic, timeless pieces never go out of fashion, and something made to last is inevitably better for the planet.

Quality Myths

Regardless of our perception of quality, there are specific indicators or ingredients of quality, that determine whether or not a piece is well-made, and will stand the test of time. Before I delve into these indicators of quality, let's dismiss some myths surrounding quality.

The Higher the Price, The Higher the Quality

Normally, you do have to spend more for quality clothing, but price alone does not equate to quality. Quality clothing costs more because it takes more time and labour to design, fit, and sew with better materials. The price you pay for a garment is not always reflective of quality, or of its sustainability. Higher prices generally mean better quality, but only if the indicators are there, like skillful construction.

In relation to price, consider the type and function of the garment, and its level of complexity. A higher price is more reliable for tailored clothing, coats, and more complex items. You'll probably want a basic item like a T-shirt to be affordable. A point is reached when an extremely expensive brand item no longer provides value. I recently saw a Prada T-shirt, without sleeves, on the cover of a fashion magazine that cost a little over $1000. An outrageous price for a basic item, when a reasonably priced Hanes T-shirt, made out of the same type of knit fabric, would serve a similar purpose. Neither is an exorbitant price indicative of quality.

Price has the power to change your perception of a product. If you are knowledgeable about fabrics and construction, you can discern if a garment is well-made and worth the expense. There are many skilled designers and manufacturers who make quality garments at reasonable price points. Price plays a part in determining quality; typically the more details added during construction, and the use of finer fabrics, the higher the price. But price is not the sole indicator of quality.

Associating Quality With Brands

You're bound to be disappointed if you buy based on brand alone. Every brand has strengths and weaknesses. There are certainly many brands that have a long tradition of specialized items, but any of these should also meet your expectations of quality, and consist of the ingredients of well-made clothing. Any brand should be able to back-up its claims of quality.

There have been many times I've felt brands to be overrated and not a worthy expense. I owned a pair of Stuart Weitzman leather boots; I loved the style, but within a short period of time the leather cracked, something that should never happen with a supposed quality leather product. Granted there are lemons in every crowd, but one bad experience is enough to alter your perception of a brand.

I've also seen quality diminish over time for brands I once purchased, and now find disappointing. My older Marks black T-shirt made out of Pima cotton and a denser knit, has stood the test of time far better than Marks newer versions. I used to purchase mid-tier brand suits, but now many women's suits are made in blended fabrics containing more synthetic than wool. Diminished quality is reflective of today's practice of cutting corners to reduce the costs of manufacturing. Regardless of the brand, carefully assess clothing purchases, particularly tailored garments, coats and leather items. They should meet your expectations, price point, and quality indicators.

All Fabrics Are Created Equally

Better materials do cost more, but as we've seen the properties of fibres that make up fabrics are different, as are the variety of woven and knit fabrics. One brand may use poor quality cashmere; whereas another company uses a higher quality cashmere in the same fabrication, but it doesn't mean these two items are going to perform the same. A poor quality fabric can't be saved by good design and careful construction. It's like saying *"all cheese tastes the same"*.

Indicators of Quality

The process of making clothes is similar to an artist creating his or her next project. Quality clothing is made with intention, and careful consideration is taken in choosing the appropriate fabric for each design, the right notions and accessories, and construction methods. Quality garments are made to last, wear well, and have a timeless, classic appeal. In assessing quality, there are four main ingredients of well-made clothing - **fabric, construction, fit,** and **details**. Today, determining quality goes beyond the garment itself, and should include where a garment is made and by whom.

Fabric

Fabric is the most important ingredient of our clothing, and determines its appearance, comfort, durability, care, and the cost. The first thing you need to do with a piece you're interested in is to inspect the garment labels, which are usually located at the neck, waist or side seam. By law in many countries, the label must indicate at least the fibre content, and care instructions. Today, shopping for sustainable materials is somewhat easier to ascertain, through a variety of certification standards for safe and nontoxic materials, recycled materials, organic sources, and fair trade products.

Natural fibres like cotton, wool, linen and silk are associated with higher quality. Lyocell or Tencel and modal are considered more sustainable cellulose-based fibres, than rayon or viscose. These days most fabric is made from blended fibres, and it is difficult to find 100% of any fibre type. The more fibres used in blended fabrics, and those which consist of more than three different fibres, are less likely blended for function or quality. A label that reads *"75% polyester, 10% nylon, 9% wool and 6% cotton"*; indicates that the minimal amount of natural fibres (wool and cotton) in this blended fabric is not going to greatly add any of their beneficial properties.

Over 65% of clothing in the market contains polyester. Today, there is too many synthetic and rayon fibres in our clothing. A brand that uses lots of synthetics and rayon in their collections, usually indicates that price is more important than quality. A line that chooses a wide range of materials is probably considering the best fabric for a garment. Activewear companies tend to rely on high-tech synthetics for performance reasons, but too much reliance is placed on the belief of comfort.

When perusing the fibre content, think about their properties, such as durability and resilience. Ask yourself questions that relate to the appropriateness of the fabric, taking into account: where it's worn, warmth, comfort, breathability, absorption of moisture, aesthetics, performance and care. Cheaper fashion is where you typically find inappropriate usage of fabrics. A densely woven polyester summer dress, will most likely be uncomfortable in the heat.

The breathability of a fabric or its ability to absorb and repel moisture is a key factor in the comfort of a piece of clothing. Synthetics do not breath because of low rates of absorption, making these fabrics uncomfortable to wear in certain climates. Newer advances in synthetic fabrications use "*wicking*" to deal with this inherent quality. Wool and cashmere, as well as other specialty hair fibres make the best sweaters for warmth, appearance, and breathability. Silk is lovely for dresses and blouses. Cotton, linen and hemp make for great summer garments.

Aesthetics or the beauty of a fabric is an important characteristic of fashionable, everyday clothing, and formal wear. Quality woven fabrics have a natural, beautiful texture and finish, and reflect light in a pleasing way. I like to play a game with myself, and guess the fibre content of a textile. I can recognize a 100% polyester suit jacket with its unnatural sheen, especially in dark colours; the fabric almost looks like glitter in the sunlight. Textured fabrics like velvet and bouclé, hang or drape in a beautiful way, that moves with the body. Silks have a lustrous sheen, because they take up dyes readily, resulting in intense, rich colours. Fabric shouldn't cling to the body, and synthetics are notorious for clinging in cold, dry climates.

Fabric has a certain hand or feel to it. High quality fabrics are pleasing to the touch. A 100% Pima cotton T-shirt is very soft, as is a merino wool or cashmere sweater. Fabrics that feel stiff and rough are probably inexpensive. Even high quality denim feels smooth and not overly stiff. Manufacturers cut costs by using synthetic fabrics, but also by using thin or lightweight fabrics. It's noticeable that fabrics have been getting thinner over time, particularly in basics like T-shirts. My older cotton T-shirts are more dense and firm, whereas some of my newer ones have noticeable thick and thin areas. Look for sturdy, substantial fabrics, unless it's supposed to be sheer or chiffon for a specific design. Thinner and loosely woven fabrics are more prone to tearing, because of fewer yarn interlacements, that make up the weave.

"Is the item durable?" is an important question to ask. The fibre type, yarns, type of weave or knit, and the stitching all contribute to a garment's durability. The function of the garment plays a role in answering this question. With high performance outerwear, durability becomes more critical than other quality indicators.

Try to avoid fabrics that pill excessively. The fibre content label will give you an idea of a fabric's propensity to pill. All knit items pill to a certain degree. The degree of pilling is affected by fibre type, yarn construction including its twist, tightness of the knit and pattern stitch. I have some very old sweaters knit in a durable, tightly twisted wool, with absolutely no pills. Pilling is common with softly spun, single ply yarns, regardless of the fibre type.

Acrylic, nylon, and other synthetics pill more than natural fibres. Silk fabric rarely pills because it consists of long, filament fibres. Because synthetic fibres are so strong, the pills don't break off the surface, whereas pills are easily removed from natural fibre surfaces. Many knitters prefer natural fibres for this reason. An acrylic item can look like *"pill central"* in no time, and the pills are almost impossible to remove from its surface.

For garments made of woven fabrics like coats, shirts and bed sheets, avoid 100% polyester, polyester blends, and microfibres. I own a wool coat with a small percentage of nylon, and much to my dismay I'm constantly removing pills. Natural fibre fabrications made of cotton, wool, or silk perform better, and any pills are easily removed. Choose woven fabrics with a tight weave. Denim items never pill, because it is made of tightly woven cotton. A beautiful silk blouse maintains its luxurious surface because long, silk fibres have high strength, and don't break off the surface like shorter fibres. Woven fabrics which are most prone to pilling, and developing a matte surface are regular rayon, fleece, and blended fabrics with a high synthetic content.

When fibres are blended together, they can shrink at different rates when washed, and lose their shape. Clothes should maintain their shape after being stretched with wear. High quality clothing has good recovery or resilience. Use fibre content and fabric structure as a guide, because poor resilience is hard to determine without wearing an item. Manufacturers do have a great deal of control over durability, beginning with choosing the appropriate fabric for the design, incorporating finishes that deal with problems like shrinkage, fading, pilling, and by testing for performance and longevity.

Note the care of a garment, and consider whether you're willing to follow the instructions. From my experience, manufacturers tend to be overly cautious when it comes to care labelling, and often indicate *"Dryclean Only"* even if an item can be laundered safely at home. Most knit items including cashmere can be hand-washed. Tailored garments, coats and 100% woven, wool trousers must be drycleaned. It is possible to wash or dryclean clothing too often, or not enough. Wool fabric repels dirt, whereas polyester and nylon are magnets for odours and stains, and actually need to be cleaned more frequently. A deeper discussion of clothing maintenance is coming up in a later chapter.

Construction Basics

The way a garment is constructed can make or break a piece of clothing. Good construction techniques increase durability, longevity, enhance aesthetics and overall quality. No matter how much I love a piece, I always check out the construction by looking on the inside of a garment, examining the threads, stitches, and seams. Clothing should look as beautiful on the inside as it does on the outside.

The thread used to sew the seams should be strong, and in a matching colour. The exception is top-stitching, a design detail used on the right side of an item. Top-stitching thread is usually thicker and more tightly twisted than regular sewing thread, and is often applied in a contrasting colour. Jeans are a great example; classic jeans use a yellow-orange thread on the outer flat-felled seams, and around the pockets. Max Mara coats have a signature top-stitching around lapels, front borders, pockets and hems. The thread thickness should also be appropriate for the fabric weight; heavy fabrics need thicker, stronger thread. Threads that break after tugging at the seam signifies low quality.

The stitches should be straight, evenly spaced, and all seam allowances should be of a similar width. It's totally acceptable for a hand-stitched item to show slight stitch variation. Generally, the more stitches used per inch, the greater the seam strength. The standard stitch length is between 8-10 stitches per inch. There are exceptions depending on the weight of the fabric; a heavy coat with a longer stitch length or fewer stitches per inch looks better, and prevents puckering.

Every step in garment construction adds to the cost of production, and that includes stitch number; the greater the number of stitches per inch, the higher the cost. Cheaper clothing typically uses fewer stitches per inch, decreasing the cost to produce. If you look closely at the seams of an inexpensive piece, and give it a tug, the seams may gather because of the fewer number of stitches, or longer length of them. Those that sew, may be familiar with long stitches or "*gathering*" stitches used in puff sleeve construction, prior to stitching the final seam. Gathering stitches are not appropriate for sewing regular seams. Avoid crooked stitching, loose threads that aren't secured, puckered seams and broken stitches.

High stress areas in quality clothing are often reinforced with an extra row of stitching, such as a second row of stitching around the inside armhole seam. Buttonholes and pocket areas are also areas reinforced with extra stitching.

High quality shirts have an extra layer of fabric, referred to as a back yoke, which strengthens the back of the shirt between the shoulders, reinforcing the back area against pulling and rubbing. Fabric patterns like plaids ideally match at the seams, requiring more work-time and extra fabric, but is visually appealing, and shows careful construction. Lower quality clothing tends to miss these kinds of steps.

Any fasteners used should be of high quality. Test that zippers move smoothly without sticking. These days, many manufacturers use invisible zippers, and if not set-in properly, they are difficult to zip up and down. I find that an invisible zipper demands holding both sides of the fabric close together along the zipper, while moving the zipper tab up or down. Exposed zipper styles can catch on fabric or jam-up with debris. A fabric placket is better option to enclose a zipper. I bought a pair of Joe Fresh jeans for $18, and the zipper broke after a few wearings; a low quality lesson learned.

Other notions like snaps, hooks and eyes, and buttons should be attached securely, and be easy to use. Buttonholes should be the correct size, so the button is not easily undone, or difficult to insert. When I make buttonholes in hand-knit garments, they are approximately 1/4 inch bigger than the button. High quality items often include extra buttons, that are attached to the inside of the garment, or provided in a separate little package. Sometimes even thread or yarn is added that was used to stitch the product. These added touches show that the manufacturer expects that a garment will be around long enough to need repairs. Good quality coats and jackets have a smaller button or piece of fabric sewn on the inside, underneath the outer front border buttons for reinforcement, preventing the fabric around the button from tearing, or getting a hole from continual opening and closing. Some finishes on fasteners can rub off, and some buttons may even dissolve during drycleaning.

Seams are what holds a garment together. Seams should be sturdy and the raw edges finished. Tug a seam gently, to reveal telltale signs of low quality, such as broken or loose stitches that make the seam prone to splitting. Most seams are pressed open to lie flat. Much of the mass market clothing is finished with sergers that cut, and form tightly looped zig-zag stitches over this edge. Serged seams are cheaper and easier to make, and is commonly used in our clothes. High quality clothing construction often incorporates wider seam allowances, needed for making specific repairs. Serged seams don't allow for garments to be made wider. Glued seams may be found in leather items. A durable garment should be held together with stitches, rather than an adhesive. Adhesives also cause problems when cleaning.

Well-made clothes incorporate visually appealing seam finishes for specific types of fabrics, such as French or Hong Kong (bias bound) seams, that fully enclose the raw edges. A pet peeve of mine is unfinished seams inside of pockets and facings. Even though these types of edges are not exposed, they should still be finished or the threads unravel over time, affecting durability.

Quality hems are folded over and stitched in place. If snagged, hems made with inexpensive thin thread often unravel. If you've experienced this, you'll notice that the thread is sometimes a clear, slippery nylon thread. I've had to re-hem many skirts and pants because of lousy thread. Poor quality hems have loose, crooked or sloppy stitching. For a classic turned over hem, the stitches shouldn't be visible on the right side. Lower quality hems are often narrow in depth, and machine stitched without extra fabric. Quality hems are stitched with no visible stitches on the right side, and extra fabric is available for alterations.

Although all hems are typically finished, some brands of men's suits leave pant hems unfinished for custom fitting, rather than having to undo a formed hem. Stitching can leave holes that are difficult to hide.

Fit

Many people equate fit with comfort, but comfort is only part of the equation. There are many people wandering around in ill-fitting clothes because they feel comfortable, but what they really mean is that they are in their "*comfort zone*". Proper fitting clothes coordinate a garment's style and structure with body proportions. Nothing looks more fabulous than well-fitting clothes, no matter what your size or body shape. I'm reminded of Ashley Graham, a "*plus*" size model strutting down the runway owning her shapely body in perfectly fitting clothes.

It's important to reference size in a discussion about fit. Women tend to get stuck on being a particular size, but the goal is to wear clothing that fits individual body types and proportions. In the past, some body types, including plus size have had more difficulty finding well-fitting clothes, but thankfully the market is changing to accommodate a variety of body shapes.

Numbered sizing (0, 4, 6, 8, 10, ...) has been used in women's clothing since the inception of ready-to-wear. It was said that women didn't want to reveal their true body measurements, hiding behind a particular number. This marketing ploy was made popular in the mid 20th century, and is still used today. Relying on body measurements is a better determination of size and fit. Men's fashion through the decades have been better at using body measurements, rather than numbered sizing. Men's suit jackets come in chest measurements like "*40 and 42*". Vanity sizing is the practice of manufacturers increasing the finished measurements of products to make a size bigger, but leave the same numbered size on the label. This marketing ploy manipulates you into thinking you're a smaller size.

Every brand determines what measurements coincide with their numbered sizes. Because there are no industry standards for sizing, a size 12 in one brand may be larger or smaller than another brand's size 12. Because there are no standards for measurements, it's easy to feel that somehow your body type is inferior. Some online fashion retailers are doing a great job of providing the body measurements that correlate with their sizes, as well as giving the finished garment measurements, which allow customers to choose a more accurate size. It's a great idea to keep a record of your body measurements to help you determine size and a good fit.

A blouse made exactly to your body measurements would be extremely uncomfortable to wear. When making a well-fitting garment, designers determine the amount of *"ease"* or fullness, so the piece fits comfortably and allows for body movement. There are two types of ease, wearing and design. Wearing ease allows for body movement. Design ease is fullness beyond the wearing ease to create a specific style. The fit of a garment can vary from very close fitting to oversized. It's possible to have *"negative ease"*. Negative ease is a measurement smaller than your body measurement. It creates a tight fitting garment, and works well for knit garments because of their innate stretchiness, which gives the fabric flexibility to fit the body comfortably.

The fit of your clothing can only be ascertained in the fitting room. Learn to examine how a garment feels and looks on your body. Can you move freely and comfortably? Can you sit down without the crotch fitting snugly? Is the waistband gaping or falling down? Does the back of the jacket pull at the shoulders when your arms are outstretched? Is your bra exposed because the front of your blouse is pulling open at the buttonhole? Does your hem ride-up or look uneven? Are the seams and darts sitting where they are supposed to be? Is the shoulder seam sitting on the outer tip of the shoulder? By viewing the garments from all angles, you'll learn what looks right and attractive on you.

Buy items that fit you now, not some place down the road, in the hopes that your body will be different. High quality brands have a consistent fit from garment to garment. You may already own garments from the same line, that you tend to purchase again and again. And if you've never had custom-made clothing, give it a try; the reward is the best fitting clothes you'll ever experience.

Fine Details

As a designer, it is the surprising details added to garments that puts a smile on my face. You may have found a special detail that makes you fall in love with a garment. It could be something as simple as a contrasting print lining inside of a jacket. Exquisitely made clothing goes beyond the basics, adding construction or design details to further enhance the beauty of a garment. A piece is made more functional, figure flattering, and a joy to wear.

With lower cost clothing, details other than the basics are usually compromised so that the item meets the desired price point. High quality garments are generous with the basics, including wide seam allowances for alterations, and any additional details are considered based on design and performance, rather than focusing on the costs to make. Fine details include garment linings, extra buttons, bound buttonholes, extra fabric at the hem, invisible hems, bias bound seams, topstitching, tailoring details like darts, fabric waistbands instead of elastic, functional pockets rather than fake ones, gussets under the armholes, and all the other fine details that craft a high quality piece.

Warranties may also be included as extra assurance that a high quality product meets the brand's standards. Warranties may include return policies, repair or replacement services, if the item doesn't live up to its expectations. My partner purchased a Canali suit, and the inside pocket contained a lifetime maintenance guarantee by the retailer. By backing up products with a warranty, a brand is standing by their high quality standards.

Who made and where is our clothing produced?

It is very difficult to understand the true provenance of our clothing, in as highly a broken and opaque system as the fashion industry. However, more companies, particularly small design and manufacturing businesses are being transparent about their manufacturing processes, and labour practices. Garment labels only provide where a piece was sewn together, without any information as to working wages and conditions, or textile production processes. Transparent fashion companies provide an important window into the conditions in which their clothing is made. Look to these businesses websites for information about their sustainable practices. This information will give a clearer picture as to how we should proceed, and to make retailers and manufacturers more accountable.

The fashion industry is global, with much of our clothing made in countries where labour is cheap. Of course not all workers in developing countries are employed in deplorable conditions, but even in the 21st century, exploitation of workers is far too prevalent in the quest for cheap labour. With an understanding of the industry, and all the work that goes into the production of clothing, one can't possibly expect quality from fast fashion or low cost clothing for the ridiculously low prices we pay.

In doing your part, buy more local, domestic, or from designers and manufacturers that share their sustainability practices. Be supportive of these companies. If we truly value the people who make our clothes, by respecting the labour, working environments, and handwork skills, our purchases will support, not exploit workers in fashion.

Quality is very different today than what it was prior to the 1990s. Fast fashion succeeded in diminishing our appreciation of fabrics and well-made clothing. Quality clothing feels amazing, is made to last, wears and fits well, and looks great for years to come. Not all of your clothing needs to be exquisitely made, but prioritize what's important to you and establish values. Learning to recognize the ingredients of quality apparel - fabric, construction, fit and fine details will help you choose better, longer lasting clothing. A classic finding in psychology is that the more effort you put into something, the more you value it. Now it's time to have some fun and construct a more conscious wardrobe.

Chapter 7

Mindful Fashion and Style

"In the rush to own things for reasons of status and looks, we lose the opportunity to be mindful and resourceful through the act of making and creating". Jane Milburn

Mindfulness

The concept of *"mindfulness"* has its roots in Buddhism, whose followers cultivate insight through meditation. Often described as an independent skill, the contemporary perspective of mindfulness supports patients and clients in helping them deal with chronic pain, illness and stress. Simply put, mindfulness is paying attention in a particular way. It is paying attention on purpose in the moment without judgement, directing your thoughts to the here and now, by focusing on the facts. There are many activities that can be considered mindful; anything that grabs your attention and awareness. The act of knitting is a mindful activity; an awareness of what's happening in the moment, experiencing the yarn and the sounds of clicking needles.

How can mindfulness be applied to fashion and creating style? Mindfulness is key to defying the instant gratification from rapid fashion cycles. More than ever, shopping is potentially addictive, exacerbated by persuasive marketing tactics, which seduce us to spend frivolously. We can practice mindful shopping by understanding our shopping habits, giving thoughtful consideration as to what we're looking for, applying textile science knowledge, and following the sustainability principles outlined in the previous chapters.

Mindfulness is central to creating a personal style, while steering clear of the negative externalities that aren't serving us or the planet. The intent of mindfulness practice is to become clear about the habits that serve you, and those that don't. Once you have a clearer focus, you can make informed choices. The ultimate goal is to create an individual style, which brings you joy and confidence, without looking like everyone else.

Sustainable Fashion

In its broadest sense, sustainable fashion refers to clothing and accessories, that are manufactured or accessed in an ecologically, and socially responsible manner. *"Eco-friendly"* or *"green"* fashion concentrates on minimizing environmental damage. Ethical fashion is more focused on the people in the fashion supply chain. To be sustainable requires a holistic approach, one that takes into account environmental, economic, and social responsibilities. Taking this kind of approach, means more than simply using sustainable materials.

Just as the designer, manufacturer, and retailer are on a journey towards sustainability, so is the individual. The important components of a more conscious wardrobe, include looking for brands, who are transparent about what is happening along their supply chain. This should be evident through the sourcing of raw materials, treatment of workers, safe use of chemicals, and other actions that show they are on the road to green. Companies that overproduce, only leads to waste. Patronizing companies that custom-make clothing, or those that produce fewer collections are great options. Other components include keeping clothes that you love and want to wear, reusing existing items, swapping, borrowing, renting, and considering secondhand as the first strategy before buying something new. Using your knowledge of textile science will help you to be conscious of the materials in clothing, and to think twice about less than optimal choices, such as recycled polyester and "*vegan*" PVC. Quality, timeless pieces are key to a wardrobe that lasts a long time.

It's certainly more difficult to find out whether a company has ethical labour standards, which is a reason to stay away from fast fashion, because there is likely exploitation going on to achieve low price points. Supporting garment workers and quitting fast fashion, recognizes and values heritage, craftsmanship, and local culture. Like companies who begin with their top sustainability priorities, articulate your values and goals, and support or patronize businesses which align with those values.

Better Shopping Habits

Alarm bells have been ringing about fast fashion's evils for awhile. What's new is the volume or scale of manufactured goods in the market. Reducing our consumption is the first step in creating a greener wardrobe. This doesn't mean substituting all of your fast fashion purchases with greener fashion. It means making a concerted effort to change the way we shop. Understanding what motivates us to shop is essential in resolving overconsumption.

Clothing fulfills the need to express ourselves, and the need to belong, which are natural human responses. People display their beliefs and values through what they purchase. In the present system, many people are dressing according to fashion trends, and what's popular with "*celebrities*" and media influencers, rather than developing an original style. Shops and e-commerce are experts at persuasive marketing from their store layouts, limited edition collections, and loyalty programs; which are key motivators in encouraging us to shop. These psychological tactics often stimulate us to buy stuff we don't need or really want. "*Retail therapy*" has become a response to emotional needs. A shopping spree is one way people deal with negative feelings, even if it's a short-lived solution.

To improve shopping habits, practice a mindful or a self-reflective approach by asking questions before shopping or at the point of purchase.

- Do I really need this piece?
- Will I want to wear this again and again?
- Is there another use, or will it work with the other styles in my closet?
- What are the materials?
- Do I want to follow the cleaning recommendations?
- Is the piece of high quality?
- Does the piece fit me well?
- Is the manufacturer practicing green habits?

Before buying new, shop your wardrobe first, by trying on clothes, restyling, repairing or tailoring items you really love to wear. Think about how you value clothes, and in this context the cost per wear. Look to quality secondhand, vintage or consignment first, before shopping new. The intrinsic nature of any fashion product is that it cycles. Fashion items come back in style, and will surly be in the secondhand market at some point. Often expensive, quality items are of better value, because over time the cost per wear is less than continually purchasing cheaper, low quality garments. I found a beautiful white cotton ruffled blouse in a consignment store for the ridiculous price of $10, and have never worn anything for as long as that blouse.

If you're really interested in a piece, take some space before you buy it. Some people devise a day rule, waiting 24 hours before succumbing. Sometimes we forget about it after waiting a bit, suggesting that it probably wasn't that important in the first place. Moving away from instant gratification, puts a kibosh on overconsumption. Made-to-order or custom work respects the time and effort that goes into making clothes.

Setting goals helps you become more conscious in imagining a wardrobe. Goal setting should be in line with personal values. This may be from a financial perspective, such as a clothing budget, or from a commitment to sustainability, like not buying synthetic fabrications. Making a list of clothing wants or needs prevents impulsive purchases. Saving up for that special something, sets up a mindset that creates joy in the search.

Habits to avoid are impulse purchases, emotional spending, shopping without a budget, giving in to that feeling of missing out, focusing on wants rather than needs, buying the same item in multiple colours, cash-back apps or other persuasive strategies. We've all succumbed to any of these habits which often leads to buyer's remorse.

Sustainable Clothing Guide

How can we incorporate a love for fashion, and maintain a unique style in a mindful way?

Know Thyself

To develop a style, begin by paring down your wardrobe. What styles and silhouettes do you like to wear - favourite styles of necklines, sleeve length, drapey or tight fitting clothes? What are your favourite colours? What items do you wear over and over? Think about what your personal style is, and what makes you feel most confident and comfortable. It may help to look at pictures of clothing styles, and the fashion of people you follow. I have a favourite photographer on instagram, who only takes photos of stylish people on the streets of different cities. This is a more realistic approach, than only citing the styles of models and celebrities. If you are stuck with too many outfits that are similar, step out of your comfort zone. Try a new look; you might find that you like it.

Developing a style is a journey, and there are many resources available on the art of style. There are also many knowledgeable professionals to help you with the process. If you stick to what works for you, you'll buy better. Don't worry about age, but don't try looking like you did in high school. Clothes should fit well, not too tight, baggy or shapeless. Having well-fitting garments makes any body shape look amazing. Express your individuality. You don't have to wear what everyone else is wearing, or chase trends. Adding creative touches, and items made by you will make your style unique.

Choose Natural Fibre Fabrications Over Synthetics

Read the garment labels for the fibre content and care instructions. Although garment labels contain a limited amount of information, they signify the properties of the fibres, which make up the fabric, and gives an indication of how it will perform. The benefits of natural fibres far outweigh those of synthetics. Synthetics are too much of an environmental problem, even recycled ones. But there is still a place for some synthetic applications, like GoreTex, a nylon based fabric that provides benefits in outerwear. Don't replace the synthetics you have with newer sustainable fibres; you still have to think about what happens to the garments at end-of-life. Items like bras, wear better in polyamide, but use silk for those special lingerie items like camisoles and slips, a luxury worth the expense. I have owned three, silk half-slips for years; lingerie pieces that are difficult to find these days.

Be wary of rayon or viscose garments. Even though rayon is a cellulose-based fibre, the manufacturing process is the same as for synthetics. There are newer cellulose-based fabrics like EcoVero, and Tencel that have a lower environmental impact, and wear better than regular rayon. Eco-fabrics are more available and labels may indicate certification standards, such as Oeko-Tex. I prefer rayon or Tencel over polyester as an alternative to silk, because of their similar properties. I would never pay a high price for a synthetic knit sweater, especially acrylic, which has a short lifespan and pills more readily, over one made of wool or other specialty fibres.

Who Made My Clothes and Production Processes

Garment workers and the environments they live and work in, are the hardest hit by climate change. Evaluating the ethics of our purchases is now more important than ever. We can't always know who's making our clothes, but more companies are transparent about their manufacturing processes, and labour standards. The fashion industry is global with the majority of our clothes made in countries where labour is cheap. It's not to say that all workers in these places are employed in terrible conditions, but in the 21st century, it's a significant problem. In doing your part, buy local, domestic, and from designers, manufacturers and artisans that share who make their collections, and how they are addressing sustainability challenges. Be supportive of these companies and shop more ethically. Don't be afraid to send a message to manufacturers for better standards. And for all the crafters, think about making some of your own garments and accessories, utilizing the variety of natural materials available. This will help you gain a greater appreciation for the process of making clothes and slow down consumption.

Quality Leads to Longevity

Quality has a different meaning for all of us, and is determined by our perceptions and expectations of what quality is. We can define with certainty what goes into the manufacture of a quality garment. The quality indicators to look for include fabric, construction, fit and fine details, outlined in the previous chapter.

Before you purchase decide how often you'll wear an outfit and where. Move away from wearing something once or only a few times. Purchase what you love, and what you'll wear for a long time. Using high quality products contributes to a reduction in fashion waste, and enhances your taste for the very reason that it is hard to find a fine piece. Quality and function are more important than quantity. As Vivienne Westwood once said *"Buy less, choose well, make it last"*.

Investment Dressing

Watch a professional stylist in action, and the phrase *"investment piece"* is part of their formula for building a smart wardrobe. Because of the times we're living in, and concerns over climate change, investment dressing makes sense. But what is it?

An investment piece is by definition a closet staple of timeless design, simple yet stylish, long lasting, and stands up to trends. Sometimes a stylist's methods for building a smart wardrobe has more to do with choosing pieces they feel are on trend, and what you must have in your closet, rather than what works for you. Just because an influencer or celebrity says you must have an item, doesn't mean it is for you.

Stylists typically run through the following list of garments, that form the basics of investment dressing: the white blouse or shirt, denim jeans, leather jackets, trench coats, black pants, LBD (the little black dress), shoes, handbags, and jewelry (gold or silver). So if you purchase a men's white shirt style, are you going to wear it? Certainly some of you may not feel like yourself in one, more like pretending to be sexy in a man's shirt. A leather jacket may not be your style or an option for vegans. What about a favourite pearl necklace? Is it really passé? Can you see the problem; these items can't possibly be universally appealing.

Dressing well and choosing investment pieces is about picking quality ones, that work with your lifestyle and beliefs, but also what will make you happy to wear each and every day. Choose one good piece from each clothing category, or more of the same styles you love wearing. I love dresses and skirts, but denim is not my idea of an investment piece. My hand-knit sweaters and scarves are some of my favourite investments, because of the time taken to make them, but also for the high quality fibres used to knit them into beautiful, textured patterns. I would never be able to find these original knits from any retailer.

The characteristics most important, when choosing invest-ment pieces are some of the ones previously discussed; lon-gevity, top quality fabrics, beautiful construction, and shopping ethically. Other characteristics include dressing for you, expressing your individuality, and what makes you feel confident and comfortable. Choose investment pieces that work well with the other clothes in your closet.

The initial cost for investment pieces usually comes with a higher price tag, and it may seem as though you're spending more. However, the cost per wear is actually less over time, than for poorer quality items that don't last. You are not sav-ing money by frequently purchasing the same type of item. Do more investment purchases for coats, suits, shoes and boots; items that are more complex, and ought to last a long time. The initial cost is normally high for a classic wool and cashmere blend coat, but the cost over time is low, in com-parison to buying an inexpensive wool, synthetic blended coat, that only lasts a season. Buying investment pieces is generally considered more expensive, with the implication of higher quality, but there is no better investment in time and creativity than making something yourself.

You Can Follow (Some) Trends

The caveat here is not to spend much money on short-lived trends. Update your classics and investment pieces with beautiful fashion forward accessories and footwear, without spending on complete outfits. It's fun to keep abreast of everything new, but remember to purchase the ones that work for you, and those you'll continue to wear, even if that means waiting for the next cycle of a trend. In our culture fashion trend cycles are not long at all.

Investment dressing for the most part is a personal journey, buying fewer things that you love, value, and which reflect your personality and lifestyle. You can break-up with the con-tinual "*must-haves*", and still follow trends without being a slave to them. Your style and your pocket book will thank you.

The R's of Fashion

There's no doubt there is an increasing awareness of the environmental effects of our choices. Using the R's is a simple model for making the most of what's already in your closet.

Reduce. This is the number one priority in dealing with negative shopping habits. Initially, decluttering is likely required, but don't simply replace the not so sustainable items with better ones. By practicing the suggestions outlined above, you'll be on the road to a greener wardrobe. You'll not only reap the benefits of saving money, but you'll create more space.

Re-wear. Normalizing re-wearing of outfits, and trying out new pairings goes a long way to ridding oneself of the one-time look. It's a slower approach to fashion, and if you really can't find what works together with items from your closet, consider clothing swaps or borrowing items that do work.

Repurpose/Reuse. Thoughtfully donate, gift or consign items you no longer want, but be wary of the potential of un-used clothing ending up in the landfill. It's possible to donate clothes directly to those in need, shelters, crisis centres, churches, and international aid organizations. Use your cre-ative DIY skills, by repurposing old T-shirts and fabric scraps into crafts, such as hooked rugs. Old wool sweaters can be felted, and cut to make new garments. Even older hand-knits can be taken apart, the yarn unravelled and reknit. Old shoes can be worn for yardwork. Upcycling is also a creative sol-ution to reusing or repurposing existing materials to produce new designs.

Repair. Previous generations were better at repairing, restoring, and salvaging clothing and accessories. Call in the professionals for projects such as alterations, reworking designs, replacing linings, and take shoes for heel and sole replacements. Keep a portable sewing kit and notions on hand for simple repairs.

Rent. This newer entry into the sharing economy is growing in popularity. Renting is a good option for those who need an outfit for a wedding or other special events, where the clothing is often worn only once. But I'm not convinced that it's the most environmentally friendly choice, since rental companies have to purchase the goods they sell, transport, package, and dryclean garments.

Resale. There are now numerous online platforms for reselling clothing and accessories. Because of the prevalent lack of attachment to our clothing, it is important to carefully consider this option. Some people actually buy more stuff to make money on the side, or they sell their purchases after a few wearings, negating sustainability efforts. Resellers are also changing the game for thrift stores, as they comb through outlets looking for bargains and the good stuff, and then sell their finds at increased prices, undercutting the stores. Some thrift store owners have started to limit resellers' purchases. This practice of reselling for profit, does nothing to reduce consumption, or to protect those who rely on thrift stores.

Recycle. Recycling is the last option in dealing with end-of-life. For now, true recycling happens with less than 1% of clothing, and most of the recycling is mechanical shredding of textiles worn out beyond repair. Technology hasn't developed efficient and clean chemical recycling systems to deal with the predominance of blended fabrics. Globally, there are a few companies that breakdown textiles, like Swedish Stockings, that produce their products from recycled materials, such as nylon tights. This company is considered a circular hosiery brand. Because of the broad definition of textile recycling, what's more common are take-back programs. Patagonia's Worn Wear program takes back used Patagonia clothing in good condition, repairs, cleans and resells it. Eileen Fisher also uses a similar strategy to keep clothes in circulation. Knickey, a sustainable underwear brand, partnered with NYC's non-profit to mechanically recycle intimates. People living in the US can box their old worn out bras, underwear and socks, and then they are shredded for use in downcycled materials. Nike has a Reuse-A-Shoe program called NikeGrinds, which take scrap materials like leather, rubber, foam, fibre, textiles, and end-of-life footwear, that are reused or processed into new materials. Some of the resulting products are new footwear, and others are a result of partnering with different companies, like for the manufacture of rubber flooring.

Less in the Landfill

We live in a world with a colossal amount of textile trash. There is more clothing than those in need. From a consumer perspective, there is a certain complexity that surrounds sorting of this waste. The complicated phrase *"textile recycling"* is somewhat of an enabler of excess consumption, making us believe that the waste will somehow be dealt with. So much of our clothing ends up tossed in the garbage, and the top priority should be to divert from the landfill for as long as possible.

Polyester and other synthetics are practically inert, and degrade at a very slow rate (hundreds of years) when compared to natural fibres. For now, making better and fewer quality purchases, keeping clothing in circulation for as long as possible, and utilizing the fashion R's can alleviate disposal challenges. Keeping clothes in circulation longer is our best solution at the moment, until at least brands, technology, and policy makers have found a way to design clothing that can be recycled back into new clothes or incorporate other end-of-life strategies.

Take Care of Your Clothes

The following chapter addresses clothing maintenance in detail. Learning to hand-wash is one of my best tips, particularly for knits, delicates like bras, and silk items. My next tip is not to dry clothes completely in the dryer. Dryer heat actually promotes wrinkling, and is damaging to some fibres. You'll also save on your electricity bill by cutting back on its use. Many manufacturers are over-cautious when it comes to care labels, protecting themselves from consumer complaints if there are cleaning mishaps. Some producers place "*Dry-clean Only*" labels on items that can be hand-washed or laundered safely. I hand-wash cashmere sweaters, and even woven, wool scarves.

There are many eco-friendly cleaning products available for a successful laundry day. Some garments must be dry-cleaned, but keep this to a minimum. You don't need to dry-clean a pair of wool pants every week or month. Depending on the amount of wear, once or twice a season is all that's required. Regular maintenance keeps clothes looking better longer.

Learn a Craft

As a backlash to fashion's lack of individuality and its design uniformity, we are embracing more traditional crafts than ever before. For all its negative attributes, the internet is a positive force in precipitating a resurgence in crafts like sewing, knitting, crocheting, and embroidery. Practicing any of these skills brings awareness to the process of making, and offers the possibility of a better relationship with clothing and its consumption. Crafting allows you to be the arbiter of taste, taking inspiration or insight from the fashion world, in developing a unique fashion philosophy. I've never received more compliments, than when I wear my hand-knit garments or accessories. Engaging in these activities is also good for your mental health, relieving anxiety, and instilling a sense of calm. And crafts can even be used as personal participation in climate action.

Consumer Activism

Major social change comes from the people inhabiting our communities. We can make a difference by divesting our resources into better alternatives, and not supporting, or enabling bad actors. Consumer activism or social pressure is what will push brands to do better. With group and community influence we can facilitate government to devise policies, providing incentive for the industry to change. Act at your level of influence, and contrary to what most people think, you don't have to be a radical activist by nature. Demanding better for the people who make our clothes, from the brands we shop in, must not be compromised.

A Note on Secondhand, Vintage and Thrift Shopping

For now, the clothes found in these types of shops is the most sustainable option for new wardrobe purchases. Shopping used is also one the most inexpensive ways to create an original wardrobe. Vintage and special consignment stores are a bit different than stores that are full of old clothes. The owners typically curate the clothing for high quality, and original fashion pieces from previous decades. The earlier looks, including clothing and handbags from couture and luxury designers, are amazing finds, which were made of exceptional materials, that took advantage of skilled hand-work, but are still less expensive than purchasing new.

There are some tips to keep in mind when shopping for treasures in these retailers. You need to spend time looking through racks of stuff to find what you want, and the willingness to try them on. Sizing has changed a lot over the years, and clothes from earlier times often fit smaller. Trying clothes on is the only way to properly check the fit. Be prepared to tweak purchases with simple alterations like adjusting hemlines or trying other creative solutions, such as cutting off jeans for a cropped or cut-off style. As you would when shopping for new items, check the condition, but for the most part garments are vetted for stains and tears. When perusing vintage, some knowledge of fashion history helps to recognize styles from the different eras.

A negative to shopping in these stores, is that their inventory depends on the city or region where you live and its demographic make-up. There are cities like New York and Toronto, that have well-stocked vintage stores, by virtue of their fashion history and large population size. Living in smaller cities, like I do, it's difficult to find high-end or luxury pieces, and the stores tend to be filled with fast fashion. I've found in smaller centres that consignment is better, as the items are curated. And most of all you have to love the search.

Some of the best quality pieces found are suede and leather coats and jackets, silk blouses, classic wool coats and blazers, wool and cashmere knits, and vintage handbags. The structured, tailored items of previous decades were of better quality. Leather vintage handbags made by artisans are timeless and special finds; you'll never find anything as well made today.

Being aware of the sustainability challenges of clothing production, and our habit of overconsumption, better fashion choices are achievable, and at the same time you can create an original style. There are many things individuals can do, beginning with knowing your personal style, choosing natural fibres and quality fabrics, patronizing brands who are transparent about their manufacturing processes and labour standards, investment dressing, and taking care of your clothing. What ultimately sets you apart from everyone else? You can be mindful, look amazing, and feel good about your choices. It's time to maintain those valuable finds, and keep them in our closet for years to come.

Chapter 8

The Goods on Clothing Maintenance

"We need to control how we care for our clothes, we need to imagine their whole lifecycle, as soon as they become ours, and plan for their future before we include them in our lives." Orsola de Castro

A mantra permeates the web. I'm not sure if it was instigated by Stella McCartney, but she is quoted by the *Telegraph* as saying, *"Don't wash clothes, just brush the dirt off...".* I admire Stella McCartney for her environmental stance, and for her design and production of high quality, sustainable fashion. She's not just talking the talk, but walking the talk. Although her quote has some truth to it, it's mostly false. The truth is brushing clothing works for certain fibres and fabrications, like wool suiting, as a method of extending the time between cleanings. But like any product we own, maintenance is key to its longevity, and part of a sustainable fashion action plan. Cleaning clothes prevents damage to fabrics, and keeps us presentable and healthy. Our laundry habits affect the environment including how we're washing, what we're washing, water usage, the release of substances into waterways, the energy utilized by dryer heat, the types of laundry products, and drycleaning methods.

Laundry Days
Why do we clean clothes?

The word "*dirt*" or "*soil*" is really a mix of a variety of substances:

- solid, particulate matter such as dust, clay, lint
- oily and fatty substances like body oils, food, cooking oil
- soluble substances like salts, sugars, starches
- colouring matter such as mustard, fruit juice, coffee, ink, lipstick

When dirt is left on clothing for extended periods of time, fabrics may be damaged, unpleasant odours build up, and soil embeds in the fibres, making its removal difficult. Regular washing maintains your clothes, and keeps them looking like new for longer. Because "*bugs love dirt*" is another reason to keep clothes clean. Insects can destroy your clothes, especially if they are stored dirty. Dirty wool can attract moths, and wet cotton attracts mildew and silverfish. These are rare occurrences, but can happen. One day at work, I was placing my bag and jacket in a locker, when I noticed a young man remove his jacket, releasing a cloud of dust (who knows what kind of dirt was in that cloud). I was mortified to think that no one had taught him the finer details of cleanliness, or how to care for his clothing.

Wash-day Blues - Effects on Fibres and Fabrics

Fibres and fabrics respond differently to water and heat. Shrinkage and stretching are common problems encountered during cleaning. Careful selection of laundry products is important, because fibres and finishes on textiles may react with their chemical ingredients. For example, bleach is a strong oxidizing agent, and damages fibres like wool and silk.

The absorbency of fibres determines how well the fabric takes up water. If a fabric resists water, like polyester does, it is more difficult to clean. Highly absorbent fibres can have their properties altered when wet. Cotton is stronger when wet, and is considered easy-care. When wet, rayon becomes more firm and increases its potential to shrink.

All fibres and fabrics are affected by temperature, and undergo damage if exposed to temperatures beyond their tolerance levels. Nylon melts if exposed to a hot iron, whereas linen tolerates high temperatures.

Colourfastness refers to the properties of a dyed textile to resist colour loss or fading, following laundering, drycleaning, exposure to sunlight, bleach, perspiration and other conditions of use. Quality manufacturers order fabrics that are generally colourfast, but it's not unusual to see some colour loss over time, or slight colour bleeding in the wash. This is one reason why it's important to separate clothes before washing into light and dark colours.

What are we washing?

In addition to the usual suspects in the wash, cotton, wool, rayon, modal, bamboo and lyocell; the majority of clothes in the laundry basket are synthetics. The prevalence of polyester, polyester blends and other synthetics negatively affect the environment with their subsequent release of microplastics. Every time a synthetic item is laundered, it releases a surprisingly high amount of microplastics into the water. Caring for synthetics is a catch 22. On the one hand they must be washed more frequently, because they are magnets for dirt and odours. And because synthetics absorb very little water, the fabric is difficult to wet thoroughly enough to assist in soil removal. So the need for frequent cleaning, with more microplastics ending up in the water system.

What can't be washed?

The care label recommends the best cleaning procedure; whether a product is washable, its heat tolerance, or needs drycleaning. For the most part, you won't have to read between the lines on labels. *"Dryclean Only"* items, include structured garments like wool suits, jackets, coats, outerwear, leather, suede, and items with special finishes, such as water-proofing. Understanding fibres and fabrics will assist you in assessing the information provided. Most knits labelled "*Dry-clean Only*" can be hand-washed successfully.

Care Symbol Guide

Care labels can be confusing and not always the ideal care methods, but they do offer at least one method of care that is safe. Manufacturers tend to be overly cautious with care label information, to deter customer complaints, and often use "*Dryclean Only*", when the item could very well be washed. Chances are that most of the clothing in your home - jeans, cotton shirts and blouses, T-shirts, socks, underwear and cotton pants are machine washable. The best candidates for the wash are simple, sturdily constructed garments with no linings, trims or structures that can lose their shape, and colour-fast items. Most wool knit sweaters, including cashmere and other specialty hair fibres can be hand-washed safely.

Symbols are commonly used in the instructions, and are often combined with brief text as to how to clean; "*Machine wash cold. Tumble dry low*". The following common symbols tell you which procedures to use or avoid when washing, drying, ironing and drycleaning.

Washing	Bleaching	Drying	Ironing	Dry cleaning
Do not wash	Do not use chlorine bleach	Hang to dry	Do not iron	Do not dry clean
Hand wash in cool water	Use chlorine bleach with care	Drip dry	Iron at low setting (110°C)	Dry clean
Machine wash in cool water at setting indicated		Dry flat	Iron at medium setting (150°C)	
Machine wash in warm water		Tumble dry at any heat or setting indicated	Iron at high setting (200°C)	
Machine wash in hot water			No steam	

Fibre Care Guide

Unless the label specifies the washing procedure for knit fabrics, sweaters, lingerie, silk and rayon, I recommend hand-washing. Sunlight damage is common with natural fibres. Synthetic fibres, particularly polyester and acrylic have excellent resistance to sunlight. Nylon degrades in sunlight. I've seen shredded nylon drapery because of exposure to sunlight.

Because much of our clothing fabric is made of blended

fibres, follow the care label carefully, and treat the fabric according to the highest percentage of fibre in the mix. Store all fabrics clean, regardless of fibre type. The following is a quick reference guide on the care for the common fibres found in our clothing.

Fibre Care Guide

Wool, Cashmere & Other Specialty Hair Fibres

Hand-wash
Cool water temperature
Fabrics labelled machine washable, use delicate, gentle or woollen cycle
Don't wring or twist
Turn inside out before washing
Use mesh bag in machine
Dimensional stability is poor; subject to felting and shrinkage
Do not use fabric softener or bleach
Do not expose to sunlight
Lay flat to dry
Steam iron by hovering over fabric without touching it, or use a press cloth on wrong side
Don't iron mohair or angora; flattens the pile
Store clean; attracts bugs, particularly moths

Silk or Silk Blends

Hand-wash
Cold water
Machine wash delicate cycle
Turn item inside out
Don't wring or twist
Do not use fabric softener or bleach
Do not expose to sunlight
Lay flat or hang to dry
Steam iron on low temperature
Iron dark colours on wrong side

Cotton

Machine wash regular or delicate cycle
Cold water for dark colours and denim
Tolerates warm water
Separate colours
Damp dry; finish drying on clothes line
Delicate T-shirts and knit fabrics - lay flat to dry
Do not use bleach
Shrinkage may be a problem
Medium iron temperature
May develop mildew; store clean

Linen and Hemp

Machine wash
Cold to warm water
100% linen tolerates high temperatures
Hang to dry or use dryer on low setting
No bleach
Iron fabric damp

Rayon/Viscose

Hand-wash or machine wash delicate/gentle cycle
Cold water
Lay flat to dry
Do not use dryer
Shrinkage may be a problem; read care label closely
Low iron
Fabric feels firm when wet

Modal

Cold to warm water
Machine wash gentle cycle
Low dryer heat setting
Do not use bleach
Behaves like cotton

Lyocell (Tencel)

Treat like rayon fabric
Cold to warm water
Tencel performs better than rayon or viscose; shrinkage is less of a problem

Polyester and Nylon

Machine wash
Warm water
Line dry
Dryer heat not recommended; use low temperature and remove promptly from dryer
Do not use bleach or fabric softener
Ironing not necessary; use low temperatures with steam
Polyester is not damaged by sunlight
Polyester attracts oil and oily stains; stain removal difficult
Redeposition problems; nylon can pick up colour and dirt; white nylon yellows with age
Sunlight exposure destroys nylon

Acrylic

Machine wash
Cold to warm water
Lay flat to dry to prevent stretching
May stretch or shrink when heated
Weaker when wet
Do not iron

Spandex (Lycra)

Hand-wash or machine wash delicate cycle
Cold water
Most elastic fabrics contain small amounts of spandex except for foundation garments, swimsuits, compression socks
Do not use dryer
Line dry or lay flat to dry
Do not use bleach, which can cause discolouration

Chlorofibres (PVC)

Simply wipe with damp cloth
Heat sensitive
Do not dryclean; PERC renders fabric brittle

How We're Washing

These days, we lack mastery of basic domestic skills from simple clothing repairs to yes, the laundry. Appliances have come a long way over the decades, and appliance makers and laundry product brands have automated the process of cleaning. We are more likely to run a quick load in the washing machine, when all that may be required is a quick spot clean. Long wash cycles aren't necessary, and a shorter wash time is sufficient for all but the dirtiest clothes.

Most washing machines found in the home are one of two types, top loaders with a central agitating mechanism, and front loaders which tumble clothes. Both types have settings for water levels and different cycles including delicate or gentle. Front loaders are more energy efficient and use less water than top loaders. Because of their tumbling action, front loaders are particularly gentle on knit fabrics and other delicate fabrications. The agitation of top loaders can be rougher on garments.

There is work being done by appliance manufacturers to develop devices that collect microplastics in the washing machine. At present, there are a variety of bags available like the *Guppyfriend* laundry bag, which hold garments while being cleaned in the washing machine. However, microplastics still need to be discarded, and may end-up in the landfill. These types of bags do help prevent the fibres from breaking off in the first place.

With advances in laundry detergent ingredients, cold water can be used for most loads. Dark coloured fabrics fade less when washed in cold water. Jeans washed in cold water keeps them from fading too much, and preserves the blue colour. I prefer warm water for washing underwear and bedding, and hot water for bath towels followed by a cold rinse. Warm and hot water does a better job of emulsifying dirt and destroying bacteria. Use the recommended amount of laundry detergent, too much won't rinse out, and too little won't clean properly.

Chances are you've experienced an errant coloured item

that found its way into a load of whites, or a wool sweater which came out of the machine small enough to fit a Barbie. Sorting laundry alleviates these kinds of mishaps. When sorting garments consider colour, fabric, and levels of dirtiness. Divide clothes into whites, light and dark colours. Sort striped clothes according to the lightest shade, so a black and white striped shirt belongs with white loads. Don't wash towels or bedding with clothing. Fabrics which produce a lot of lint should be washed separately from those that attract lint, to reduce pilling. Wash heavier fabrics separate from lighter weight and delicate fabrics. Ideally all denim clothes get their own load.

Pre-treat stains and odours. This can be as simple as soaking or spot cleaning items in a small amount of detergent and water before hand. Do not use hot water when washing blood stained items or the blood sets into the fabric permanently. Collars and cuffs of shirts should be gently scrubbed with the chosen pre-treatment.

Place delicate fabrics, items that may snag and synthetics in a laundry or mesh bag before placing in the washing machine. Empty pockets; nothing is worse than Kleenex breaking up in the wash. Close zippers and turn most clothing inside out before washing. Wash new coloured clothes alone, to protect other clothes from any residual dye released in the wash. I use the gentle cycle for most of my clothing. Towels and bedding can tolerate normal machine cycles.

Use the delicate or gentle cycle of the washing machine for machine washable knits. Some front loaders come with wool and silk washing cycles, which have lower spinning speeds. I lay out knits flat to dry on a towel covered blocking board, a knitter's tool used to pin out hand knit pieces as they are finished, which helps to even out stitches and flatten edges. You can simply layout sweaters and other knits on towels over top tables or the floor to dry.

Dryers are the most energy intensive step in the laundry process. We use the dryer too much. Limiting dryer times, saves on your electricity bill by cutting back on energy. A short dryer time for items like no-iron shirts, fluffs the fabric and helps to stave off wrinkles. I only completely dry bath towels, and partially dry bed linens. I damp dry most machine washed garments on low or medium heat for a few minutes, then hang or lay flat to complete drying. Dryer heat promotes wrinkling, and is damaging to some fibres like spandex. Compression socks contain high percentages of elastic and should be line dried, as well as other items with high amounts of spandex.

Dry full loads at lower heat settings. Synthetics don't belong in the dryer, as they air dry very quickly, and generally don't tolerate heat. I find there is less wrinkling and minimal ironing required when clothes are smoothed out and hung up to dry after only a few minutes in the dryer. Make sure to clean the lint filter after every load.

Line drying outside is not as common as it once was. I remember my mother line drying outside, even in the winter time (frozen towels, not so great!). There are many varieties of indoor, foldable lines for air drying in the home. In addition, I use a rolling garment rack to hang garments like shirts, blouses, T-shirts, and pants. Take out as much moisture as possible before line drying. Hanging up sopping wet clothes may stretch them out of shape.

Direct sunlight can fade certain fibres and fabrics, especially natural fibres like wool and silk, and dark-coloured fabrics. But sunlight UV rays are a bleaching agent, and kill germs quite effectively. Whites can be naturally bleached this way.

Hand-Washing

Hand-washing clothes is a task that most people would rather avoid, but is really an easy and convenient way to clean. Of course anything that can be machine washed can be hand-washed. Most hand-knits and other knit fabrics can be safely washed by hand. Some items labelled *"Dryclean Only"* can be hand-washed safely including wool, cashmere and silk fabrics. Bras, lingerie, and many rayon viscose fabrics are best hand-washed. Most wool and other hair fibres are easily washed by hand. If you aren't sure about whether something can be washed, do a spot test in an inconspicuous area like an inside seam, and see how the fabric reacts. Shrinkage is most often caused by heat, and the fabric will react by puckering. Wool labelled as *"superwash"* can be machine washed, but I prefer to hand-wash these kinds of wool fabrics. Many items that have decorative embellishments such as sequins, beads and ribbons are best hand-washed. Suede, leather, velvet, fur, and structured jackets, coats and suits need the expertise of a drycleaner.

How to Hand-Wash

Fill a sink or basin with room temperature or cool water, and add a small amount of mild soap specially made for delicate fabrics. In a pinch, a clear dishwashing liquid such as Ivory will clean very well and is not expensive. Place the item in the soapy water and let it soak. I let wool or other hair fibres soak for 30 minutes, and silks or rayons for 20 minutes. Squeeze gently, swishing the suds through the item, focusing on necklines, cuffs, and armholes, or the dirtiest areas. Drain the sink, pressing the garment towards the side of the sink or basin. Rinse with cool water 2 or 3 times, or until the water runs clear. Squeeze excess water out, but don't twist. A trick for removing water from sweaters is to place the item into an old pillowcase, tying the top of the case loosely so the item doesn't fall out. Mesh laundry bags used for washing delicate items also work well. Place in washing machine, and briefly spin out excess water on drain/rinse cycle. For lightweight cashmere and merino items, or items with embellishments roll in a towel to get rid of excess moisture. Lay the item flat on towels, shaping and smoothing to its original size. After mohair or other fluffy knits are dry, air (no heat) fluff them in the dryer to raise the pile.

How Often to Wash

We should be washing less often. Before tossing clothes in the washing machine, ask yourself whether items are indeed dirty or smelly. Don't be swayed by online blogs listing the exact number of wearings before cleaning. Common sense applies, taking into account hot weather, accidental spills, and odours that tell you it's time to wash. Clothing that sits next to the body, underarms, below breasts, feet and crotch require frequent washing. Underwear, socks, hosiery, and swimsuits should be cleaned after every wear. Whites may need to be cleaned after each wear, like white shirts that attract dirt at cuffs and necklines. Hand-wash bras after about 3 to 4 wears. Leggings, shapewear and gym clothes after 1 to 3 wears, unless you notice odours or tend to sweat a lot.

For other types of clothing, keep an eye out for dirt and stains. I usually attend to coats and outdoor jackets at the end of the season. Wool sweaters and cardigans, again seasonal, unless the knits are worn close to the body. Most clothing can be left a little longer without problems.

Synthetic garments that trap soil and odours, need more frequent cleaning. Also the type of synthetic garment dictates when to clean, a polyester dress needs less cleaning than synthetic athletic wear. Because synthetics need more frequent cleaning, this is a good reason to limit the amount of synthetics in your wardrobe, and build one mostly around natural fibres. Protect outer garments with underwear or under-layers, to minimize the amount of cleaning.

Extend the Time Between Cleanings

The following methods extend the time between cleanings, have a gentler footprint, and are simple procedures to add to your routine. If your garment isn't that dirty, or an accident happens, spot clean as soon as possible before the stain sets. Blotting with a little water should be tried first; water may be all that's required. If you need some cleanser, try water and a dash of clear liquid soap, and gently brush to work out stain. I keep soft toothbrushes and clean rags to deal with stains. Rinse with clean water by blotting with a wet rag. More detail about stain removal is coming up in laundry products section.

Dry dirt and lint responds well to brushing with clothing or lint brushes. Brushing works great for wool suits, tweeds and many structured garments which require drycleaning. Wool repels dirt, making it easy to brush off dry dirt sitting on the surface of the textile. I'm not a fan of adhesive lint rollers, as they can leave behind residue. Brush garments after each wearing, before storing them in the closet or drawers.

Before placing clothes back into the closet and for optimal freshness, hang them up to air out. Portable steamers are handy for travelling, or simply to refresh clothing at home. The steam also helps to minimize wrinkling.

How to Deal With Those Annoying Pills on Your Fabric

Is your favourite sweater covered in pills? We've all experienced those unattractive, fuzzy balls on the surface of sweaters and other textiles. These balls of fibres are called pills, which are short fibres or fibrils entangled on the surface of a textile. Pills result from abrasion or friction. Abrasion occurs in areas of heavy wear, such as cuffs, inner side of sleeves where the arm rubs against the body, and the heels of socks. Pilling is a frustrating problem, but there are some preventative measures to reduce pills, and some nifty tools for removing them.

How to Reduce Pilling

A little fabric knowledge and some practical steps can help to reduce pilling:

Check fabric labels. All knit items pill to a certain degree. The degree of pilling is affected by the fibre type, yarn construction including its twist, tightness of the knit fabric, and the pattern stitch. I have some very old sweaters knit in a durable, tightly twisted wool, with absolutely no pills. Pilling is common with softly spun, single ply yarns, regardless of the fibre type. Acrylic, nylon, and other synthetics pill more than natural fibres. Because synthetics are typically strong, the pills don't readily break off the surface. For this reason, pills are more easily removed from natural fibre textiles, than from synthetic ones. An acrylic item can look like *"pill central"* in no time, and in extreme cases develop a matted looking surface. I own a wool coat with a small percentage of nylon, and much to my dismay it pills. For garments made of woven fabrics like coats, shirts, and bed sheets avoid 100% polyester, polyester blends, and microfibres. Natural fibre fabrications made of cotton, wool, or silk perform better, and any pills are easily removed. Choose woven fabrics with a tight weave. Denim items never pill, because they are made of cotton and tightly woven. A beautiful silk blouse maintains its luxurious surface because silk fibres are long, have high strength, and don't break off like short fibres.

Remove any pills before cleaning. Preparing the surface of the textile before cleaning helps to prevent further pilling.

Wash smarter. Sort laundry by colours, as well as by fabric types. Don't wash towels with your delicate items, or mix high lint producing fabrics with ones that attract lint. Turn sweaters and other clothing inside out, to prevent abrasion caused by contact with other items. Because the washing cycle is not that gentle, especially in top loaders, hand-wash knits and other delicate garments and fabrics.

Dry carefully. A dryer too full of clothes, can cause them to rub against each other, and leads to pilling. Limit the dryer time, leaving clothes damp, and hang them up or lay flat to finish drying. Don't put synthetics in the dryer. Sweaters, delicate clothes, or items that may stretch, lay flat on towels to dry.

Pill Removers

De-pilling works best on natural fibre surfaces. Synthetic fabrications that are heavily pilled may also have a matte looking surface, and the pills can't be removed without damaging the textile. Have you ever tried to remove pills from microfibre tights after a season of wear - doesn't work, the balls are there forever. Here are some common pill removers, and the list includes some you many not have heard of.

Fabric Shavers. These devices shave off the pills from the textile surface. I've never used one, but likely works best for woven fabrics. I would avoid them for hand-knits.

Sweater Stones. These are blocks of pumice that are rubbed along the fabric surface to remove pills. I was not happy with the results when using a stone, because of the pumice residue left behind. There are different brands of stones available that may work better.

Fabric and Sweater Combs. I've had one of these for years, and it works great on fine gauge sweaters. It's gentle and doesn't damage the knit fabric. I've also used it on woven fabrics like wool coats, with good results.

Personal Razor. Recently I tried a disposable razor on my wool coat and it worked well. Don't use a razor with many blades, or those infused with lotion (common sense prevails). I wouldn't use a razor on a hand-knit; the knit fabric may be snagged or damaged.

Lice Combs. This tool was a surprise, but with its widely spaced metal teeth, it works for bulky knits covered with large pills. Simply comb through the pills to remove. That being said, if you have nothing better to do while watching TV, you could remove large pills by hand.

Pills on a fabric can range from none to a matted, unsightly surface. However, with some preventative measures, avoiding synthetic fabrications, and using a pill remover, your garments will look better, and you'll wear them much longer.

Laundry Products

Water is critical to the cleaning process, and is characterized as either soft or hard. The hardness or softness of water affects the sudsing and cleansing action of soaps and detergents. Hard water consists of a high percentage of calcium and magnesium minerals, and their concentration varies with the source of the water. High amounts of these minerals leave a residue on textiles. Soft water is preferred for cleaning textiles.

Water conditioners are used to soften hard water, and today many detergents contain conditioners or softeners, rather than having to add a softener to the water along with the cleanser. In the past, Calgon powder softener was often added to the wash water. In locales where hardness is a problem, soft water systems may be combined with water tanks in the home. Cleansers create more suds in soft water than hard water, and require smaller amounts of detergents.

Cleansers are used to remove dirt from the fabric and hold it in suspension in the cleaning solution. There are different types of cleansers: soaps, synthetic detergents, and plant-based more "*natural*" cleansers. Soaps are not as common anymore, and work best in soft water. In hard water, soaps can leave an insoluble residue on clothes. Synthetic detergents are the classic petroleum- based cleansers in the market, like original Tide. They are highly alkaline and very good cleansers, but over the years companies have modified their ingredients because of environmental concerns.

Green household cleaning supplies have been around for years. Many of the major brands carry eco-friendly product lines which contain plant-based ingredients. Natural and fragrance free options are available, which don't contain chemicals like chlorine bleach, dyes, or colourants.

Laundry detergents come in powders, liquids, pods, tablets, and eco-strips that contain biodegradable surfactants or cleansers. They are made specifically for front loaders (HE labelled) and top loader machines. Because of the concerns over plastic waste, which comprises the packaging of the majority of laundry products, eco-strips are a great alternative. Some brands provide refillable options, a great solution to reduce plastic and packaging waste. Be wary of detergent pods because they have been found to contribute to plastic pollution, leaking PVA (polyvinyl alcohol) into the environment, and potentially into the human food chain. The marketing claims of *"biodegradable"* pods are questionable, and it hasn't been proven that they completely breakdown in solution. A common problem is using too much detergent, and because of the high concentration of products today, a very small amount is enough to do the job.

Bleach is a whitening agent and is not a cleanser. Oxidizing bleaches are used to whiten, brighten, and remove stains. Bleaches used in household laundering are either chlorine or non-chlorine (perborate). Hydrogen peroxide is a mild perborate bleach. Chlorine bleaches (Purex, Clorox) are strong, more powerful whitening agents than perborates, but can damage fibres and finishes. Chlorine bleaches may also cause yellowing and dye fading. Chlorine damage occurs with specific fibres, including all protein fibres (wool, silk), and spandex. If chlorine bleach comes in direct contact with any dyed fabric prior to dilution in water, the dye leeches out and you're left with a splotchy fabric. Accidental spills are common and ruins a perfectly good item. Perborate bleaches present fewer problems, but may not whiten as effectively. I would stay away from chlorine bleaches because of their harmful effects on fabrics and the environment.

Pre-treatment products such as Shout and OxiClean are used to effectively remove oily body soil that collects on areas like cuffs and collars, and other stains such as blood, lipstick and wine. These treatments contain enzymes and other chemicals which are potentially toxic. Liquid detergent, shampoo, laundry soap bars, or a paste of laundry powder work as well as pre-treatment products, and are useful for pre-soaking heavily soiled or stained items.

There are many eco-friendly treatment products made by a variety of companies. An arsenal of common household products including vinegar, baking soda, clear liquid dish soap, rubbing alcohol, and hydrogen peroxide are effective stain removers, that are safe and non-toxic. There are many sources available on how to remove stains, using these simple household ingredients. Blot stains instead of pushing into the fabric, and gently scrub when using a brush. Spot cleaning and stain removal just takes a little effort and patience.

I like OxiClean (hydrogen peroxide) for stubborn stains, if water and soap doesn't work. Don't give up after the first attempt; try a different method, and avoid the dryer, as heat will set most stains. Two different stains may be present, and each may require a separate stain removal method.

Vinegar is also a great softener and freshening product to use in the rinse cycle, and no your clothes won't smell like pickles. It also gets rid of soap residue, and dilutes excess suds. Dye bleeding during hand-washing is not uncommon, particularly with dark dyes, and adding a little vinegar to the rinse water helps to stabilize the dye.

Why I Don't Use Fabric Softeners
There's a commercial on television, a marketing faux pas, which has very little truth to it. It goes something like *"When your V-neck looks more like a U-neck, you know your T is half-washed.....Downy will prevent stretching...."*. Well, I lose it because you can't reverse damage, aka stretched fabric, and what does half-washed mean anyway? I'm going to give you the goods on fabric softeners, and why you shouldn't use them. Fabric softener is one of the most over used household product. Our use of fabric softener is usually due to a desire for scented clothing, but its use comes at a

cost - to us and to the environment.

What is fabric softener?

Like the conditioner used on your hair, fabric softener is a conditioner for your clothes. Fabric softeners are a mixture of chemical compounds, that form a thin, waxy, water resistant film on the surface of the fabric. The coating binds static charge, rendering the fabric with antistatic properties. It also imparts a softer, fluffier feel to the fabric, reduces wrinkle formation, and adds fragrance. Fabric softener is commonly found as a liquid which is added to the rinse cycle, or as dryer sheets. Most dryer sheets are small pieces of synthetic fabrics coated with fabric softener and other toxic compounds. There are now "*natural*" dryer sheets available but the jury is out on their environmental effects. Other products for those obsessed with long-lasting fragrance include in-wash scent and softener beads, as well as fabric sprays.

The Problems With Using Fabric Softeners

There are harmful effects caused by using softeners. The Allergy and Environment Health Association has found that fabric softener is the most toxic product made for daily household use. They contain a cocktail of petroleum based chemicals, toxins, carcinogens, and allergens harmful to humans and the environment. Although we love the smell of fresh laundry, the fragrance in fabric softeners is a common cause of irritant dermatitis in sensitive individuals.

Using fabric softeners increases the flammability of fabrics, or makes clothes more flammable. This is the reason labels read "*Do Not Use Fabric Softeners*" on children's sleepwear, and flame resistant fabrics. The flammability is increased as much as seven times.

The coating imparted on the fabric also lessens its ability to absorb water, and actually makes clothes more difficult to clean. Fabric softeners should not be used on towels, as they become less absorbent over time.

Fabric softeners are harsh on natural fibres like pure cotton or bamboo, and decreases their absorption rate. Fabric softeners leave a residue that dulls the finish on clothes which contain elastane (lycra or spandex), and attracts odour causing bacteria. Fabric softener poured directly on synthetic garments in the washing machine will leave oily stains, and isn't easily removed.

If this wasn't enough, fabric softeners are bad for washing machines and plumbing. They form a *"scud"* in the machine, clogging pipes that forms a breeding ground for bacteria, encouraging the growth of mold. If you use fabric softener, the washing machine must be cleaned regularly with vinegar or bleach. The earlier dryer sheets produced by manufacturers caused a build-up in dryers, which was difficult for technicians to address.

Softener Alternatives

Fabric softener sheets tossed in the dryer are popular, because they infuse scent, eliminate static and minimize wrinkling. But the classic dryer sheets pose too many harmful effects. You can make dryer sheets at home, by cutting cotton cloth squares infused with a few drops of your favourite essential oils. Foil can be scrunched into a ball, then tossed into the dryer for static control. Felted wool dryer balls are a great option for softening and preventing static.

Better Softener Substitutes:
- 1/2 cup of baking soda should be added to the wash cycle. Baking soda is a great deodorizer, and enhances the cleansing action of laundry soap.

- 1/4 to 2/3 cup of vinegar should be added to the rinse cycle. Vinegar is good for getting rid of soap residue, as well as ridding the washing machine of buildup. Don't worry, you won't smell vinegar in your clothes.

- One of the many recipes available for homemade fabric softener involves combining 6 cups of vinegar, 1 cup of baking soda, and 10 drops of essential oil in a glass jar. Use 1 cup per load of laundry.

- Fabric sprays and fresheners. Most of the fabric sprays in the market contain toxic chemicals, and softeners. These types of products are also being made by companies that manufacture natural laundry products. Fabric sprays and fresheners are not cleaners, they only mask odours. It is easy to make a freshening spray at home, and one that is often recommended is one part vodka to four parts water. This will deal with cigarette smoke, perfume, and light body odour.

I hope I have made you think twice about using fabric softener. It is an unnecessary laundry product, and there are far better substitutes. My best tip is to reduce dryer time to stave off wrinkling, or eliminate its use and hang clothes up or lay flat to finish drying. Natural, common household ingredients, mainly baking soda and vinegar offer similar benefits as fabric softeners. Felted dryer balls are fun to make (no knitting required) and how-to instructions are found online.

When Soap and Water Won't Do - Drycleaning

Drycleaning is necessary for some items in your closet, and extends the life of high quality garments. Dryclean items like wool coats, jackets, suits, and evening wear once a season unless very dirty. Spot clean as needed. Leather is easily wiped, but the lining is usually what gets the dirtiest; let the lining dictate when cleaning is necessary. Wearing scarves prevents collars from getting too dirty. The cleaning process is termed drycleaning because little or no water is used; organic solvents replace the water needed to expel dirt.

Limit the use of traditional drycleaners, which use toxic chemical solvents. The most widely used non-flammable solvent is PERC or perchloroethylene. PERC's fumes are toxic and carcinogenic. If you notice a residual odour of PERC on drycleaned garments, this is an indicator of poor quality and low standards for the process.

Drycleaning is often thought of as a trouble-free method of caring for clothes. There are problems that may arise such as shrinkage, colour changes, redeposition of dirt, solvent residue, and a loss of hand and body. Don't send PVC or imitation leather items to the drycleaners, because vinyl plastics leech out in presence of solvents, resulting in a hard, brittle substance. Polystyrene plastics used in some buckles, buttons and sequins may dissolve in solvent. Remove any precious buttons and special fasteners before drycleaning. There are eco-friendly or green drycleaner options that don't use the classic chemical solvents. Ask the company what solvents they use and their toxicity.

Some people take items like men's shirts to be laundered and pressed at the cleaners, but often their washing and pressing methods are harsh on fabrics. When we were on vacation many years ago, my partner had one of his shirts washed by the hotel cleaners, and shockingly it came back with shredded areas.

Ironing

Ironing is not one of my favourite tasks. Decreasing dryer time alleviates wrinkling and the need to iron everything. But laundry rooms would be amiss without a good steam iron, even if it isn't used that often. I typically iron shirts, blouses, or very wrinkly garments. Irons are handy for touch-ups to keep clothing looking their best between cleanings. Refer to care labels for the proper settings or correct ironing temperatures appropriate for the fabric. Synthetics typically don't need pressing, and are damaged by high temperatures.

Use a spray bottle of water to dampen any fabric made of plant fibres, like cotton and linen. The moisture ensures a crisp finish. Pressing cloths are helpful when ironing dark coloured fabrics, as the heat from the iron can leave shiny marks. Press dark coloured fabric on the inside, rather than the outside of the garment. Old tightly woven, white napkins or dish towels make great pressing cloths. Use steam on knits and woollens without touching the fabric, hovering the iron closely over top. And if you happen to take-up sewing, the iron is essential for minor repairs, pressing seams open, and finishing.

Many newer irons are anti-drip, as leaks can leave water stains on delicate fabrics like silk. Empty the iron after each use, and regularly clean the iron according to the instructions. Buildup of water minerals can leave deposits on fabric.

How to Iron a Shirt or Blouse

A cotton shirt or blouse is a staple in most wardrobes, and usually requires ironing. A good iron has multiple heat and steam settings. Use a sturdy ironing board, and take your time, using long, slow passes of the iron. Cotton fabrics usually tolerate higher heat settings with steam. Here are the steps to ironing a shirt without tears:

- Spray the shirt generously with water. Roll it up and let the water permeate the fibres for a few minutes.

- Begin with ironing the underside of the collar. Try not to pucker the fabric by gently pulling and stretching the fabric away from the iron.

- Iron the back yoke, the extra fabric at the top back of the shirt, moving the shirt along the curved end of the ironing board as you press.

- Iron the left front buttonhole (men's style) band on the inside, then turn shirt so the left front lies on the board right side up. Go over the band again.

Ironing a Shirt

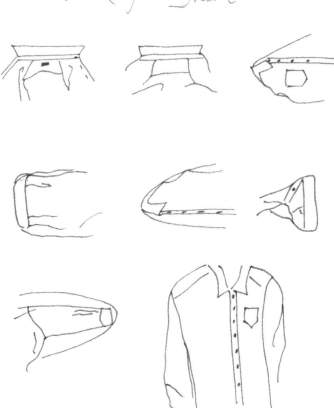

- Iron the fabric, moving across the shirt, from the left front, across the back, to the right front, finishing with the right front button band. Move the tip of iron between the buttons to smooth the fabric.

- Sleeves may be ironed on a sleeve board, but I smooth out the sleeve as you would when wearing it flat on the board, and move the iron over the whole sleeve. I do the cuff last by ironing the inside, then the right side.

- Hang up shirt on the appropriate hanger, and do up the top button, and you're done. Perfection is not required.

Storage

Cleaning clothes, followed by proper storage is key to clothing's longevity. Proper storage maintains a garment's shape over time. The clothes you're wearing right now are typically hanging in your closet, and some are placed in drawers or shelves. There are a variety of hangers from which to choose, each with a specific purpose. Padded hangers keep lightweight blouses and lingerie in shape. Hangers that come with clips or clamps leave trousers and skirts looking crisp and wrinkle-free. Wooden hangers are my favourite and are practical, keeping coats, jackets, suits, and shirts in shape. Because of their shape, wooden hangers allow space between garments to prevent overcrowding that may lead to creases. Flocked hangers are useful for items that tend to slip off wooden hangers, such as silk blouses or lightweight trousers. Be wary of garment hooks, which may cause misshapen necklines and stretched areas. Some garments like housecoats have a loop of fabric stitched into the neckline so the item can be hung on a hook.

Different styles of boxes and dividers fit inside of drawers to hold items like socks, underwear and T-shirts. Sweaters and cardigans are best folded and placed in drawers, rather than hung, which causes them to stretch out of shape.

Clothing should be stored cleaned, particularly when storing garments for the season. Because bugs thrive in dirty, humid environments, cleaning textiles before storing is essential. Some fibres and finishes are unable to resist damage by insects, microorganisms, and mildew caused by humidity. Generally, storing clothes in cool, drier environments minimizes attack.

Stains not removed before storage may permanently set, or become more difficult to remove as garments age. Exposure to sunlight can cause yellowing and deterioration. Some fabrics can even shred after long exposure to sunlight. Be careful of direct sunlight in the spaces where you hang or store clothing uncovered. It doesn't take long to notice sunlight damage.

Off-Season Clothing Storage

If you have space in your closet, move off-season garments to the back of the closet or off to the side. However, an overstuffed closet makes it difficult to see what your choices are. By removing items you won't be wearing anytime soon, you can choose clothes more easily, and keeps you from wearing the same items over and over again.

Before packing away off-season clothes, it's a great time to edit your wardrobe. Edit by subjecting items to a quick assessment: Did I wear it enough? Is it still in good condition? Is it time to donate or resell? Are any repairs necessary?

Seasonal clothes should be stored clean in breathable containers, like fabric-lined boxes or archival boxes, which are acid-free. Plastic bins are okay, but some types of plastics leave odours, so dryer balls infused with a drop of lavender oil, cedar blocks or sachets placed inside the container keeps clothing fresh.

Folding and Storing Your Precious Knits

Storage of knits, especially sweaters is often done improperly. It freaks me out when retailers hang sweaters on garment racks, because of the potential for stretching. Sweaters are better folded and placed in a drawer or other type of container, rather than hung.

Watching Marie Kondo in action is a mindful experience. She's the queen of decluttering and organizing living spaces, but with a twist - she wants you to experience the joy of having only the things you love around you. All the hard work, joy and time you put into knitting a sweater, or the high cost paid for a purchased one, caring for it guarantees a long life. You'll notice that Marie Kondo folds most clothing items into neat bundles that easily store away, and take up less space in your drawers and closets. Let us "*Kondo*" our sweaters.

Before storing knits, make sure there are no visible stains, and address needed repairs. This doesn't mean your knits must be washed after every wear, but they shouldn't be visibly dirty. Do any necessary spot cleaning, and air out garments after wearing, then store. Store knits flat, and loosely stack them. Tissue may be placed between garments to allow air to circulate. I like to place tissue inside the folded sections of fine weight knits and cashmere items.

Some knits may require moth protection; moths are attracted to dirt, skin oils, and animal proteins. Yarns with high levels of lanolin and natural oils, like minimally processed wool are susceptible to moths. With this in mind, you may want to separate knits for seasonal storage into those that attract moths and those that don't. Plant fibres like cotton, and synthetics aren't damaged by moths. Most yarns produced today are treated to prevent damage by moths. I've never encountered garments damaged by moths, but have seen the damage inflicted on museum textile artefacts. Lavender sachets and cedar blocks work well stored along with clean knits, to keep moths at bay. Remove garments that have been drycleaned from plastic bags, and air out to remove any residual solvent odours before storage. Don't store items in plastic drycleaner bags.

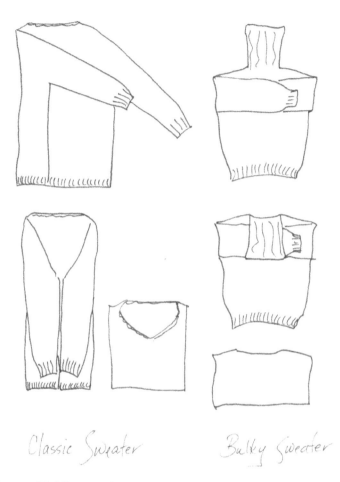

Classic Sweater   Bulky Sweater

How to Fold

Folding knits is the best way to store them. Garments placed on hangers can stretch, and make marks or points at the shoulders.

- **Light to Medium Weight Sweaters**. Place your sweater face down (frontside) on a large surface, and smooth out any wrinkles. Fold one side of front toward the back, then fold the sleeve down. Follow the same procedure on the other side. Fold the sweater in half, bottom up. For fine gauge knits, you can place a piece of tissue inside the folded sides before the sleeves are folded down. For garments with front closures, like cardigans, do up all the buttons before folding. For garments with no front closures (ie. wrap cardigan), I fold with the back face down instead of front down, so the fronts remain closed when stored.

- **Chunky/Bulky Sweaters**. Place sweater face down, turn in one sleeve, then the other. If there is a turtleneck, fold it over the folded back sleeves. Fold the sweater in half. This reduces bulk, and they stack easier.

- **Using a Hanger The Right Way**. Here's another method of folding a sweater over a hanger to store in a closet. Fold sweater in half, vertically, and line up the sleeves. Lay the garment on a flat surface. Position a hanger (wood, plastic or flocked style) with the hook between the arm and body of the sweater. Wrap the sleeves over shoulder of hanger, and tuck under the lower bar. Repeat with body of sweater. Sweater hung but folded!

I place knit and woven accessories including scarves, shawls, hats, and socks neatly folded in fabric containers. I separate summer and winter accessories for seasonal storage. Hats stuffed with tissue helps to maintain their shape. Taking a little time to fold and store garments in an organized fashion will add a longer life to those precious hand-knits. After all the effort knitters and crocheters put into making them, why not put some effort in caring for them.

Be Skeptical of DIY Hacks

Marketing advertisements at their worst present information that is either completely false or deceptive. A great example of this is a television ad subliminally promoting synthetics, but is expressed as a *"truthful"* rhetorical question;

"Did you know 70% of your clothes are synthetics?... Woolite takes care of all types of...". The internet is also filled with DIY hacks for fixing the endless number of household problems, some worthy of trying, some not so much. A comment from a reader of *"Wool and The Gang's"* Instagram feed, says that putting wool sweaters in the freezer *"cleans"* them; a claim worthy of skepticism. But a DIY fix that caught my eye was a solution for fixing shrunken sweaters in the November 2020 issue of *Real Simple Magazine*. Researching this claim online led me to many hacks on stretching not only knits, but other clothing including jeans and T-shirts. These fixes defy my knowledge of textile science.

The Fix

The recipe for fixing a shrunken sweater made of wool or cashmere is to soak the item for awhile in warm water with a small amount of olive oil, fabric softener or baby shampoo. After the soak, remove it from the water bath (no rinsing) and roll in a towel. Place on a towelled surface, and gently stretch to its original size. Let the sweater dry and its shape *"should be"* restored.

The Facts

Fabrics composed of natural fibres like wool, cashmere, mohair and cotton are subject to what is called progressive shrinkage - the fabric shrinks a bit more with each laundering. This happens with wool because of felting shrinkage. This is why wool is hand-washed in cold or room temperature water without twisting or agitating to preserve the integrity of the fibres and prevent shrinkage. Superwash wools are treated to prevent felting, rendering the knits machine washable. Felted fabric does not stretch because the fibres are set in an entangled, matted state. So a sweater that has felted will not stretch from exposing it to this type of treatment, in fact you may even felt the item further.

Blocking is an essential step in the finishing of knit projects. It's the process of wetting or steaming knit pieces, or completed projects to even stitches and fibres, flatten edges, and "*shape*". Some resources inaccurately describe stretching the pieces to a "*correct*" size. No amount of stretching will change a garment's size, and may damage the knit fabric. If your sweater has shrunk to a "*doll*" size there is no going back, regardless of what you do.

Wool fibres and other specialty fibres are resilient, and respond best to blocking or shaping. However, if your sweater is made of cotton yarn, which is less resilient than wool, stretching a cotton sweater will likely cause it to lose its shape. Wet blocking synthetic sweaters, like those made of acrylic yarn will not change the nature of the fibres because they don't absorb water; this fix is useless for these types of fabrics.

Shrunken sweaters already have a lot of stress placed on the individual fibres. Over stretching these sweaters further subjects fibres to more stress and makes them less durable. There is also the potential to rip seams by pulling the item tightly.

I wouldn't want to risk further damage of a wool or cashmere sweater. One solution is to gift it to someone it now fits. On the other hand, if the reality is a shrunken sweater, I guess it might be worth trying the fix to see if you can get a little more life out of the sweater.

Many of these types of hacks are deceptive, as there are many caveats placed on the fix. There is certainly disappointment from a pre-loved wool or cashmere sweater having found its way into the washing machine. There is no possibility that you can "*unshrink*" a favourite garment, and I would rather see it have a longer life on someone who can wear it.

Mending Matters

Your "*slow fashion*" journey would be remiss without learning a few simple stitches to make minor repairs. It's a way to care for what you already have in your wardrobe; deepening a relationship with clothing, the essence of sustainable fashion.

Common repairs which are easy to accomplish include: sewing on buttons, stitching a fallen hem, patching torn areas of garments, and darning a small hole in a sweater or other knit. Mending is satisfying and fun, allowing you to be creative in your approach, and upcycling items you love that have seen better days. A sewing machine is not required, just some hand sewing techniques. Even haute couture relies mainly on hand-sewing skills which distinguishes it from ready-to-wear.

There are many great resources and classes for learning basic hand-sewing methods. The basic stitches to learn include **straight or running stitch**, useful for attaching patches or decorative details in contrasting colours. The **whipstitch or overcast stitch** is great for joining edges of fabric. **Backstitch** is a strong, secure stitch, that is used to close a split seam, and for specific seams in hand-knit garments. Finally, a **hemming stitch** such as the blind hem fixes a fallen hem. Each of these basic stitches are easily found online or from your favourite sewing resource.

Denim jeans are perfect patching projects, extending the life and usefulness of your beloved pair of jeans or other denim pieces. While we're talking about mending denim, distressing your own jeans by fraying or deliberately making holes, adding decorative patches, or any other embellishment such as sewing on beads, appliqué or embroidery is far more fashionable and greener than what you'll find in any retailer.

Buttons are easy to attach onto garments. Buttons come in different types; sew-through or flat buttons with either 2 or 4 holes, and shank buttons which are raised above the fabric. Thread shanks can be added to raise sew-through buttons while stitching, to allow movement and prevent pulling and tearing of the fabric around the button.

Sew-through Buttons
(either 2 or 4 holes)

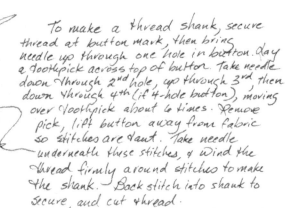

To sew button flat to a garment take several small stitches to mark button location, then center button over the marking, and sew in place through holes in button. Fasten stitches on wrong side or between garment and facing.

Sew button flat, only on very thin, light weight fabrics, or as a decorative button.

To make a thread shank, secure thread at button mark, then bring needle up through one hole in button. Lay a toothpick across top of button. Take needle down through 2nd hole, up through 3rd, then down through 4th (if 4-hole button), moving over toothpick about 6 times. Remove pick, lift button away from fabric so stitches are taut. Take needle underneath these stitches, & wind the thread firmly around stitches to make the shank. Back stitch into shank to secure, and cut thread.

More often, add a thread shank, which permits the closure to fasten smoothly & will keep fabric from pulling & tearing around the button.

4-hole buttons can be sewed on in different ways to form a cross, square, other shapes, or simply 2 parallel lines.

Shank Buttons

For fabrics that are not very thick, make enough small stitches through fabric and shank to make button secure. Threads should be parallel to the opening edge.

To make an additional shank, hold forefinger between button & garment, and bring thread several times through shank & back of fabric, creating space between stitches & fabric. Tightly wrap thread around stitches to form the additional shank. Fasten thread securely on underside.

Put together a sewing kit or basket containing a variety of needle sizes for different types of fabric, straight pins, tape measure, scissors, seam ripper, and common thread colours (white, black, navy, brown), adding other colours as needed. Use a container to hold extra buttons. Once you've tried the basic stitches, you might find yourself wanting to learn more advanced sewing skills.

Get to Know the Neighbourhood Tailor and Other Professionals

Not all of us are so inclined in attempting minor repairs, or unable to reimagine changes to our garments. Unfortunately, repair professionals are not as common anymore, but with a little research and asking for recommendations, you will find an expert. Many drycleaners offer basic repairs and alterations. I've used a skilled tailor for years, who was initially recommended by a retailer.

Tailors and other professionals address the classic problems, such as open seams, broken zippers, adjusting hemlines, taking in or letting out seams, and replacing lining fabric. A good tailor can perform more complex repairs, such as narrowing shoulder width of jackets, which often require removing the lining, and realigning a patterned fabric. If you're not sure of a professional's skill level, have them do a simple repair, and then assess it. Also take into account how they relate to you, how they communicate the problem, and the solutions offered.

The majority of clothing bought off-the-rack are in standard sizes, and will rarely fit us perfectly. This is another reason to utilize a professional tailor who can alter a garment to fit you. Sleeves that are too long, or a waistband that hangs loosely, are easily altered by a skilled professional. A good tailor can even redesign a piece, such as changing a neckline style.

Repairs and alterations can be pricey. Others disagree with me, but I believe a garment must be well-worth the expense.

Many fast fashion items aren't worth making complex changes. Poor quality clothes often don't have enough available fabric in the seams for specific kinds of alterations. But cheap clothing is great for upcycling projects or other creative solutions. Complex alterations should be saved for special items. By learning the basic skills outlined above, you can perform minor repairs without the expense of a tailor's expertise, regardless of the price you paid for something. Upcycling clothes just warrants a little creativity; I've sewn fake pearls onto jeans, and embroidered areas on knits and blouses.

Care of Shoes and Leather Accessories

High quality leather footwear, if taken care of, can last many years. Cobblers or shoe repair experts are more difficult to find than tailors, because of a declining interest in repairing footwear. The most common shoe repairs are heel replacements, resoling, and preserving shoe toes with toe taps or half soles. I find that once I replace the original heels, which are often made of plastic material and quickly wear down, the new ones last much longer. Fasteners like zippers can be restitched in place. A cobbler can assess whether or not an item can be repaired, and as with clothing, leather repairs can be costly, so quality special items are more worthy of the expense.

Basics of Shoe Care

The longevity of footwear depends on the amount of use (a lot of walking), the wearer's gait characteristics, and the weather. Athletic footwear and inexpensive shoes have shorter lifespans than quality leather footwear. Tips on caring for leather footwear:

- Use insoles like Dr. Scholl's inside shoes and boots to protect the footbed.

- Rotate your footwear, and use shoe trees, or stuff the toes with tissue.

- Remove white, salt residue and dirt from footwear as soon as possible. There are many cleaning products, plus non-toxic ones that work well. Even a damp cloth dabbed in vinegar removes salt.

- Polish regularly.

- Don't wear the heels down completely.

- Don't walk on the backs of your shoes.

- Toe taps, particularly on women's pointy-toed shoes protect from damage.

- It is optional to spray footwear with protector, and is usually applied before first wear and prior to seasonal wear. Make sure you read the instructions before use.

- Store seasonal footwear by cleaning, and stuff toes with tissue. I like to store shoes in their original boxes, but there are a variety of other ways to store footwear, if you have the appropriate shelving and space in the closet.

Leather handbags simply require a regular wipe with a damp cloth. Many high quality luxury bags recommend not using leather conditioner or sprays which can mark or leave stains. Store leather bags in a fabric pouch or in a fabric lined box. High quality leather items often come with special fabric bags. I'm a leather glove person, and I wipe these as well with a damp cloth at the end of the season, and place them in a fabric container.

Craftfulness

After trying your hand at mending and repairing, you might find yourself interested in learning a needlework craft. Since my teens, I've delved into many crafts and sewing projects, but knitting is my passion, and has been part of my work life as a designer, helping others execute their ideas for hand-knit collections. It's the needlework crafts that directly impact a fashion wardrobe. These skills include sewing, both machine and hand-stitching, embroidery, knitting, crochet, patchwork, and many others.

The original Arts and Crafts Movement began in the late 19th century as a response to the industrialized manufacturing of household goods and clothing. Handmade clothing and other crafts became popular, prioritizing the skills of artisans. Like the Arts and Crafts Movement, knitting was revolutionized in the late 1980s by Kaffe Fassett, an artist and needlearts expert. Since the early 2000s social knitting has rekindled an interest in knitting among young people, both male and female, firmly planting the craft. Knitting is here to stay. Today, knitting is serious business, evident by the knit collections of many designers.

The point I make here is that learning and practicing a craft benefits our well-being, develops an appreciation for handwork skills, and the time and effort that goes into making clothes. It is also a satisfying way to make our wardrobe more sustainable. I knit the majority of my sweaters and accessories like scarves. The best part of making something with your hands is you get to choose the best quality materials, and reuse or repurpose materials. You gain an appreciation for the time and effort taken to create something with a greener footprint.

For me, nothing is more satisfying than freshly laundered clothes and clean, polished shoes. And nothing can keep me from knitting each and everyday. These acts may seem more like chores and mindless activities, but they come with quick and sustainable rewards. Learning to care for your most personal possessions is not only fulfilling, but is a small, achievable change, which has a more profound impact on the environment than you may think.

Last Words

"Consumer demand can revolutionize the way fashion works as an industry. If everyone started to question the way we consume, we would see a radically different fashion paradigm." Carry Somers

Is there a saying you absolutely hate? The phrase that makes me cringe is *"It is what it is"*. It's true there is a certain reality to any situation or crisis, but for me this phrase implies that there are no solutions, and we just have to live with things the way that they are. The reality now is that fashion companies who embrace traditional, capitalistic business models, prioritizing profit over people and the planet, have only succeeded in perpetuating overconsumption, environmental destruction, and exploitive practices.

As a whole the industry suffers from a lack of sustainability, transparency and accountability, with many companies including luxury brands producing volumes of disposable clothing, leaving a host of environmental and human costs in their wake. Clothing is one of many consumer products we buy that is designed and manufactured to drive excess consumption. For too long, manufacturers have downplayed quality, valuing quantity and low price. Most consumers don't know what a quality garment should look like, and we live in a world where clothes don't live long enough to be old.

Fast fashion has erased what clothing and style mean, diminishing clothing's value and knowledge about its origins. Dressing in our clothes is supposed to be a personal and individual act of expression. Today, fashion has become more about status, rather than wearing an interesting piece or revealing an artistic individual style. But realities can change.

The challenge for companies is about striking a balance between profitability and sustainability. This is difficult to achieve because there is an inherent conflict between the pursuit of profit, growth, and sustainable principles. In recent years, there are many examples of brands that have made progress in developing different types of business models, which strike a better balance between economic viability and achieving sustainable goals. Mass production can't be eliminated but problems can be fixed.

More localized manufacturing is one such solution. Although this type of production may not be scaleable, it is easily replicated and indeed viable. Growth can be small and steady, with better designed, quality offerings that focus on solving fashion's footprint challenges. Investing in circularity includes increasing the durability of garments, providing warranties, offering repairs and promoting reuse. The manufacturers of our clothing is where the process of change begins. Policy will be the main mechanism that forces change through the support from brands to improve transparency and circularity within the industry, and create a more diverse, competitive advantage for all sustainable companies.

Here we are at the end, but it could be the beginning of a new way of approaching a world over-saturated with clothing, and our compulsion to continually buy. Becoming a more conscious shopper of fashion is the easiest place to begin making our contribution to developing a more sustainable fashion industry. This book will be a success if I have managed to entice you to reflect on the clothes hanging in your closet. Look at them differently. Knowledge of textile science, understanding quality construction and the properties of good fabrics, as well as all of the work involved in textile production, will help you visualize the long journey it takes for garments to reach point of purchase. Once you understand what goes into the production of clothes, your view will change. You can't help but see the value in your clothes, and you'll know if your money has been well spent. Have the courage to develop your own style. Buy the best, flattering well-made clothes you can afford, make good use of them, and care for your treasures. Reject the aggressive marketing strategies that drive us to purchase things we don't need. Give up the clothing deals and steals. No matter what the price, subject all purchases to a quality assessment, and your sustainable principles. We can incentivize manufacturers to do better.

...

I live in Alberta, one of the western provinces of Canada that has seen unseasonable heat and drought conditions over recent years. This spring is unprecedented, with one of the worst wildfire seasons ever recorded. In fact, all of Canada and areas of the United States are blanketed in smoke from fires, which have ignited even in areas never having witnessed this type of devastation. I'm writing this final chapter early this morning, because I'm unable to go outdoors for my regular walk, because the Air Quality Index is 7, or at a high health risk. These extreme wildfire conditions and high temperatures are the result of a warming climate. The main culprit of these intense events is our addiction to fossil fuels. There is no doubt that the fashion industry has greatly contributed to the climate crisis, alongside all the other industries that comprise our modern world. And now, its effects have landed on our front doorstep.

With the wildfires forging their destruction across Canada, I don't know what more we need to see to act. Climate change stands between us and our future. We can't just turn off the switch, but we can accelerate radical change, even in an industry as complex and seemingly frivolous as fashion. What better place to start than by realizing the true value of our clothes.

Glossary

Capitalism is an economic system in which private individuals or businesses own goods. Capitalists or business owners employ workers who receive wages to produce goods on behalf of the owners. Under capitalism the production of goods and services is based on supply and demand in the market or market economy. Capitalists choose where to invest, what to produce and sell, and at which prices to exchange goods and services. The profit motive is the driving force of capitalism.

Circular design is a process that aims to produce and consume goods while generating as little waste as possible. Products are designed for durability, reuse, remanufacturing, and recycling; while seeking to improve the environment by lowering waste and emissions. Not much of our modern fashion industry is circular, and about 1% of discarded clothing is recycled into new clothing.

Closed-loop system is a manufacturing approach which rethinks and redesigns the way products are made and discarded, or rather embraces circularity. Waste and pollution are considered in the design process and minimized or eliminated. The materials and products are designed to be reused, repaired and remanufactured. Closed-loop systems regenerate material systems. The production of Tencel fibre is considered a closed-loop system; the solvent used is more easily recoverable, and almost no solvent ends up in the eco-system.

Consumerism is an economic and social system perpetuating the belief that by increasing the consumption of goods and services purchased in the market is desirable for a person's well-being and happiness. In a pure economic sense, consumer spending is a key driver of the economy. In capitalistic economies, excessive consumption has led to a host of environmental and social problems.

Fashion is a complex term carrying wide meaning and affected by many factors. In the context of this book, fashion refers to the apparel products created by designers and accepted as a popular form of dress at any given time, and admitting all the variations that exist due to social class, occupation, status, wealth, and personality inherent within the concept of "fashion".

Fashion industry encompasses a variety of industries, all concerned with the design, manufacture, and distribution of textiles, women's, men's and children's apparel and accessories.

Fast fashion's development begins in the late 1980's with the globalization and logistical efficiency of production processes. Fast fashion brands loosely interpret designs of others, and manufacture clothing and accessories in inexpensive fabrics and low quality construction, without the fine details and skilled techniques used to make high-end clothing. Low cost offshore manufacturing allows these companies to release trends quickly through large quantities of inventory and low prices, while realizing high profits.

Historic costume is a study of clothing or the style of dress or costume peculiar to a nation, class or period of time. An understanding of clothing's history views clothing as a means of communicating personal and societal values within a specific historical period. "Fashion" arose during the late Middle Ages as a response to a changing society and technological developments.

Linear business model (cradle-to-grave) is one that designs products in a one-way process, whereby resources are extracted, made into products, sold and eventually disposed of, usually in a landfill or incinerator. Unfortunately, linear models dominate modern manufacturing, and focuses on making a product and getting it to customers quickly and cheaply without considering much else.

Marketing can be defined as being a process to plan and execute the conception, pricing, promotion and distribution of ideas, products or services through an exchange that ultimately satisfies the consumer and the company involved.

Needlework encompasses decorative hand sewing and textile crafts that utilize a variety of needle types for construction. Needlework includes embroidery, needlepoint, knitting, appliqué, quilting, patchwork, macramé, crochet, rug-making, and lacework such as tatting.

Product lifecycle defines the way every consumer product moves through the market. A fashion product or trend cycle refers to the process of introducing and popularizing a new trend. The fashion product lifecycle moves through five stages: introduction, rise, acceptance, decline and obsolescence. In today's fashion industry, these product stages are all present, but we're cycling through the stages at an incredible pace, fueled by fast fashion and now ultra-fast fashion. Because fashion products and trends work in cycles, trends often return. Historically, trends would maintain popularity much longer, around 3-5 years, but now they cycle through in months or weeks.

Regenerative agriculture is a way of farming that focuses on soil health. Globally, the land used for crops has been degraded by the effects of intensive farming, from the use of machinery, pesticides and fertilizers. Investment in regenerative agriculture is the latest trend in fashion production, but it's only one solution in reducing pollution caused by the fashion industry.

Slow fashion is the anti-theses of fast fashion. Slow fashion is typically a mindful approach that slows down every stage of fashion's lifecycle. Generally, slow fashion brands produce small intentional collections, promote conscious shopping habits, design long lasting durable, quality products, and are mindful of their environmental footprint. Businesses tend to be more localized with products made in smaller workshops, and are transparent about their supply chain. Slow fashion does overlap with sustainable principles, but not all slow fashion is sustainable. Because a garment was made slowly, doesn't mean the fabrics were sourced responsibly or workers paid fairly.

Textile is defined loosely as any product made from fibres which are woven, nonwoven, or made through other manufacturing methods such as knitting. Traditionally, "textiles" only referred to woven fabrics.

Textile science studies textiles used in the production of clothing, home furnishings, home accessories, as well as in the manufacturing of building products, protective apparel (firefighters and farming), transportation products and geotextiles. The field of textile science plays an essential role in our physical environment. Textile scientists are concerned with the components and properties of fabrics.

Ultra-fast fashion includes online retailers which are even "speedier" than fast fashion outlets. For some ultra-fast fashion companies, new collections are dropped daily. Ultra-fast fashion takes everything bad about fast fashion, and pushes to the absolute extreme: high volume, faster fashion cycles, low prices, synthetic fabrications, and negative impacts on workers and the environment. The popular ultra-fast fashion brands include Shein, Fashion Nova, Boohoo, Pretty Little Thing, and Cider.

Bibliography

Bravo, Lauren. *How to Break Up With Fast Fashion*. London: Headline Home, 2020.

Canadian Broadcasting Corporation (CBC):
The Current. Ultra-fast Fashion. May 3, 2022.
Marketplace. Hidden Price of Your Clothes. Season 49, Episode 6, November 5, 2021.
Spark. Fashion Futures. 516, September 10, 2021.

Caulfield, Timothy. *The Science of Celebrity*. Toronto: Penguin Canada, 2020.

Clement, Brian R.; Clement, Anna Maria. *Killer Clothes*. Summertown, TN: Hippocrates Publications, 2011.

Cline, Elizabeth L. *Overdressed*. NY: Portfolio/Penguin, 2012.

Cline, Elizabeth L. *The Conscious Closet*. NY: Plume Penguin Random House LLC, 2019.

Corner, Frances. *Why Fashion Matters*. London: Thames & Hudson Ltd, 2014.

Cunningham, Patricia A.; Voso Lab, Susan. *Dress and Popular Culture*. Ohio: Bowling Green State University Popular Press, 1991.

Davidson, Rosemary; Tahsin, Arzu. *Craftfulness*. London: Quercus Editions Ltd., 2018.

de Castro, Orsola. *Loved Clothes Last*. UK: Penguin Random House, 2021.

De La Haye, Amy. *Fashion Sourcebook*. London: Quarto Publishing plc, 1988.

De La Haye, Amy; Tobin, Shelley. *Chanel The Couturiere at Work*. Woodstock, NY: The Overlook Press, 1994.

Gross, Valerie. *Fashion Design Companies in Alberta: Factors Affecting Viability and Competitiveness*. Degree of

Masters of Arts, Edmonton, Alberta: University of Alberta Press, Fall, 1998.

Hoskins, Tansey E. *Stitched Up*. London: Pluto Press, 2014.

Johnston, Amanda; Hallett, Clive. *Fabric for Fashion: The Complete Guide*. London: Laurence King Publishing Ltd, 2014.

Kassatly Veronica Bates; Baumann-Pauly, Dorothee. *New Report: Greenwashing Machine*. eco-age.com: Geneva School of Economics and Management, September 15, 2019.

Kondo, Marie. *the life-changing magic of tidying up*. Berkeley: Ten Speed Press, 2014.

Laver, James. *Costume & Fashion*. London: Thames & Hudson, 1969.

Lobenthal, Joel. *Radical Rags*. NY: Abbeville Press, 1990.

MacKinnon, J.B. *The Day the World Stops Shopping*. Toronto: Vintage Canada, 2022.

McDonough, William; Braungart, Michael. *Cradle to Cradle*. NY: North Point Press, 2002.

Milburn, Jane. *Slow Clothing*. Australia: Textile Beat, 2017.

Parkes, Clara. *The Knitter's Book of Yarn*. NY: Potter Craft, 2007.

Patel, Rupal; Meaning, Jack. *Can't We Just Print More Money?* The Bank of England. Penguin Random House UK, 2022.

Press, Claire. *Wardrobe Crisis*. Australia: Nero, 2016.

Rodabaugh, Katrina. *Mending Matters*. NY: Abrams, 2018.

Rouse, Elizabeth. *Understanding Fashion*. Oxford: BSP Professional Books, 1989.

Routh, Caroline. *In Style 100 Years of Canadian Women's Fashion*. Toronto: Stoddart, 1993.

Sax, David. *The Future of Analog*. NY: Hachette Book Group, 2022.

Schuman, Scott. *The Sartorialist Man*. NY: Rizzoli International Publications, INC., 2020.

Shaeffer, Claire B. *Couture Sewing Techniques*. The Taunton

Press, 1994.

Siegle, Lucy. *We Are What We Wear*. Guardian Shorts, Audible Studios, 2014.

Stephens, H. *The Industry Itself*. Canadian Business Special Issue 24(4), 24-26, 84, April 1949.

Thanhauser, Sofi. *Worn*. New York: Pantheon Books, 2022.

The Economist. *Reinventing Globalisation*. June 18th, 2022.

Thomas, Dana. *Deluxe*. NY: Penguin Press, 2007.

Thomas Dana. *Fashionopolis*. NY: Penguin Press, 2019.

Tortora, Phyllis; Eubank, Keith. *A Survey of Historic Costume*. New York: Fairchild Publications, 1989.

Printed in the USA
CPSIA information can be obtained
at www.ICGtesting.com
JSHW070233220324
59542JS00014B/115

9 781554 835485